Eliminate Your SDBs

D1052364

Eliminate Your

SDBs*

Jonathan M. Chamberlain

*Self-Defeating Behaviors

Brigham Young University Press

Library of Congress Cataloging in Publication Data

Chamberlain, Jonathan M. 1928–
    Eliminate your self-defeating behaviors.

    1. Conduct of life.   I. Title.   II. Title: Self-
defeating behaviors.
BF637.C5C47   158†.1   77-27634
ISBN 0-8425-0998-4

To Beverly, Lori, Chuck,
Lisa, Mark, David,
and all others
who would be happy.

Contents

Preface

At nineteen I was struck down and mauled by our jersey bull on my father's farm in Kanab, Utah. A few days later as I was regaining consciousness from having undergone an exploratory abdominal operation, a voice awakened me from my anesthetized sleep. The sound of that voice and the one simple question it asked have remained with me to this day: "When are you going to write your book, Johnny?" In that instant my eyes opened to see my tired, watchful mother dozing in a chair nearby. It was not her voice that spoke to me.

In the almost thirty years since that incident I have searched for "my book" to write—one worthy to be written, one that would hopefully bring more dignity and purpose to the lives of others. Perhaps this is the book I was to write.

Acknowledgments

This book would not have been possible without certain basic concepts by Milton R. Cudney (1971), who has generously allowed me to take his ideas and implement them in my own way to help others. His unpublished paper, presented at a convention in 1971, contained steps for this change program, the concepts from which I have tried on myself and my clients with positive results. (Chamberlain, 1973, note 1.) Cudney provided an innovative format for a group therapy in which an individual group member's problem could be kept confidential and in which the individual could nonetheless be helped. He devised a simplified method of attacking almost all behavioral-emotional problems by pointing out how, in many respects, they are similar in origin and how they are similarly maintained in our lives. He brought together a great variety of prominent theories of counseling and therapy into one simplified, easily applied but powerful pattern for one's changing his or her behavior. This pattern, once learned, can be applied over and over again to eliminate all of one's self-defeating behaviors.

While I am thanking people for their help, I must thank the two clients on whom I first tried this method in 1971. One was a minister who worked through his temper tantrums; another was an educator who overcame his fear of speaking in public. Their willingness to try this new method and their success in making changes apprised me for the first time of the benefits inherent in this method.

I am also indebted to my friend and employer, Burton C. Kelly, Ph.D., director of the Counseling Center at Brigham Young University, for his encouraging me to research and conduct group workshops and to counsel individual student clients using this method. I am also indebted to other colleagues at the Counseling Center for their suggestions, support, and participation in ESDB workshops—both as trainees and leaders.

I am grateful for the many graduate students who have contributed more knowledge regarding this method through their research projects, theses, and dissertations. Their scholarly works are cited in the introduction.

I am indebted to Ronda Ferguson and the secretarial staff at the Counseling Center for helping me prepare the manuscript. Thanks are also due to the many students in the live workshops and those pioneering the home-study approach using this method.

The BYU Home Study Office personnel under Mack Palmer and Ron Malan need a special thanks for their foresight in encouraging me to develop a home study course entitled "How to Eliminate a Self-defeating Behavior." (Chamberlain, 1976, note 2; BYU Bulletin, 1977; 35, 152.) This course has been successful in reaching many people in other parts of the world and in aiding them to eliminate some of their self-defeating behaviors.

Thanks go also to Leora Thurman, director of BYU Campus Education Weeks, for encouraging me to expose this method to many thousands who attend that annual event.

I extend deepest appreciation to my wife and family for their willingness to have an absentee dad long enough for me to get this job done.

Introduction

Most of us search throughout our lives to find effective ways of overcoming self-defeating habits or ideas we have acquired in the process of maturing. All this searching is aimed at finding lasting happiness within ourselves in an ever-changing society and usually leads us into external programs that hold a promise of that special help we seek. We sometimes give these external ideas power over our lives. Often, the more we do this the more we are dissatisfied with ourselves and the less happy we feel as we try to fit ourselves into another person's criteria for happiness, so that when the helping program ends, unless we have made its concepts a part of our lives, we may grow more distrustful of self and of any other program that claims to help. One of the tragedies of this never-ending search is that we fail to recognize and use the great powers already within us to achieve the very happiness we seek.

There is much evidence to indicate that we are capable of experiencing a greater degree of happiness when we have learned to discipline ourselves enough to discover our real selves by gaining or regaining control over behavior patterns. When we know where we stand with ourselves and have learned how to recognize and be in charge of our own thoughts, feelings, and actions, each day can be filled with a zest for living. This feeling for life is hard to imagine when you have not felt it, just as it is hard to imagine life without it when you have.

Through our lives we tend to maintain many unnecessary and burdensome recurring thought and behavior patterns. These patterns keep us in a constant state of misery so that we dare not hope for a moment of respite or for anything like permanent freedom. We become emotionally, physically, and sometimes socially crippled by these burdens.

It was not always so with us. We came into this world as innocent babes and, psychologically speaking, we were created with no hang-ups. Cudney tells us that "man is inherently cooperative, unique, constructive and trustworthy, and when he is free of defensiveness [and other self-defeating behaviors] his actions are positive, forward moving, and constructive." (Cudney, note 16.) When we were still tiny infants, our minds, like busy computers, took into our mental and emotional systems thousands of bits of information per minute. Although we may have since slowed down, we have not stopped yet, nor will we; for learning seems to be an ongoing process. (Moody, 1976.)

In each fresh moment of time we absorb new experiences and sensations and knowledge. We are continuously at the threshold of being our better selves. We are kept from it only by the personal choices we make in those moments of time. Although our choices may be colored by our past, when we learn how to take charge of the moment and the choices we make in it, we are free from confusing influences. These choices are colored and influenced by the present life circumstances in which we find ourselves; but even here, we can so order our own circumstances or our perception of them so that our lives are enhanced rather than defeated by them.

You, then, were born into this world psychologically whole and complete, but in the process of growing up you learned certain behaviors necessary to cope with life situations. Some of those learned behaviors became self-defeating to you as you continued to do them over and over again, inappropriately, long after the original situation no longer existed. Fortunately, you have learned a greater number of self-enhancing behaviors than self-defeating ones, or you would not be as well off as you are now. You were created to function well without any self-defeating behaviors; yet in our world it is almost impossible for a human to mature without picking up one or more behaviors defeating to human potential and to a successful life.

I am sure that by now you are wondering how this new "freedom" can be achieved, won, or experienced (or whatever it is you do to get it). That's what this book is all about—learning how to gain freedom from your self-defeating behaviors, but in such a way that you know what you are doing and that *you* are in charge. A self-defeating behavior is any recurring thought, feeling, or action that in some way keeps you from being the fully functioning person you could be. A more complete definition will be given later.

2

In spite of your past record of failing to overcome a self-defeating behavior pattern in your life, you will find this method to be easier than you might suspect. As it usually turns out, people make it as "easy" or as "hard" for themselves as they seem to feel the need to. As you will see later, we all have ways of doing this.

You may be wondering also, "Because this is an external method or program how can it get 'inside' me so that I know I will have it there even after completing this book or applying your program? How do I know I will not revert back to my old behavior pattern or way of thinking even when I have completed the program? I am not certain I want to risk failing again at trying to give up this defeating behavior pattern in my life. I cannot take many more failures. They are defeating to me as a person and definitely do not help to achieve happiness."

These are normal concerns, and the answers will be forthcoming. This program is based on principles you can test out for yourself, apply immediately, and continue to apply in your life long after you have completed this change program. In addition, you will discover that your freedom to choose or not to choose your self-defeating behavior is greatly enlarged; whereas, at the present time it may seem to you that you are not free to *not* do it. You have likely determined many times *not* to do your self-defeating behavior, but at the first opportunity you have done it again in spite of your resolve.

You will find that all behavior is meaningful and purposeful, and when you examine closely how it functions in your own life, you can then exercise greater care to achieve the goals you truly want for yourself. You will also discover that everyone has one or more self-defeating behaviors. I am reminded of this when I look at the avoidance techniques—such as cleaning my office, then my typewriter—I was tempted to use to put off a little longer writing this book.

The self-applied principles of behavior change presented here have been scientifically researched and reported (Chamberlain, notes 3, 4; Bills, note 5; Bohn, note 6; Coombs, note 7; Fiester, note 8; Forsyth, note 9; Hendricks, note 10; Jacobs, note 11; Johnson, note 12; Parks, note 13; Parks, et. al., 1975; and Seamons, et. al., note 14). They are based on concepts related to several major theories in psychology and counseling (Berne, 1961; Ellis, 1973; Glasser, 1965; Krumboltz, 1969; Maslow, 1968; Perls, 1969; Piaget, 1961; Rogers, 1961; Stampfl, note 15; and Wolpe, 1966). These concepts, hopefully, are written in a personable and understandable way so that almost anyone can learn them and apply them.

3

Some readers have thought it difficult to believe that the same instructions and methods could apply to so many differing behavior patterns ranging from deviant, aggressive sexual behavior and other forms of violence to feelings of timidity and shyness. After many years of experience as a psychologist, I sometimes find it hard to believe myself. If it were not for the beneficial results of hundreds of experiences with participants in private and group settings (and even through home study, done totally by correspondence), I would not believe it possible either.

These many experiences, along with research my colleagues and I have done, lead me to believe this method is based on some common and sound ideas. But these ideas take personal and consistent application in our daily living in order to be beneficial to us.

We will refer to this method for eliminating self-defeating behaviors as the *ESDB Program,* a seven-step process designed to provide you with techniques and personal assistance to help you eliminate behaviors that are self-defeating to you.

Specifically, my objectives for you in this program are as follows: 1) to take you through a step-by-step process designed to eliminate self-defeating behaviors; 2) to help you demonstrate your control over a self-defeating behavior through your actual application of the concepts presented; and 3) to help you experience living without your self-defeating behavior. The result for many participants has been a discovery of the real self as a person of greater worth and dignity and the casting aside of an old and erroneous self-image.

This book was *not* written to be read once and put aside and forgotten. You may do that if you *choose,* but by so doing, you will know that you have avoided getting down to the important self-understandings you were seeking when you selected this book to read, a book I have written to help you make changes in your life that will bring you greater joy. There will be ample opportunities for you to apply the ideas presented.

The ideal schedule for reading, making personal application, and completing this program is a four-to-six-week period, allowing you time to experience catching yourself doing your SDB and to do some relearning about it. To derive maximum benefit, follow directions carefully and take only one step at a time. If you do this, I can promise that you will achieve success in changing, if not totally eliminating, your problem behavior—in spite of yourself.

This book is totally self-contained, so that everything you will need is included in it. Think of it as a workbook to be used or a handbook in which to write.

4

In a way of speaking, you are going to help me individualize and make personal this ESDB program so that it will fit your needs. When you have completed the program, you will have in your hands a set of tools you may use until you run out of self-defeating behaviors.

I arrived at the point of writing this book in several stages. I began the ESDB program in 1971 with two of my private clients. It worked for them in overcoming stuttering and temper tantrums. I tried it on myself, and it worked for me in overcoming my inability to say "no." I tried it with groups of university students; it worked there. I tried it with inmates at a state prison; it worked in that setting. I tried it with school teachers and administrators in district workshops, and many of them have never been the same since; it worked for them. I tried it in marriage counseling; it worked there (but *only* when each one was willing to assume responsibility for his or her own behavior). My colleagues and graduate students have tried it with upper elementary school children, junior high students, middle school children, and high school children; it worked for them. I have used it in private practice with a variety of adult problems; it has been a success there, too.

Then I discovered that it works even for people who are geographically distant from me, through home study. The success resulting from this unique way of helping people has led me to dare believe that many more people could experience the same benefits from this totally self-contained program without professional assistance. Thus, whoever you are, you are participating in a pioneering adventure with me. The challenge this idea presents has spurred me on to write this book.

It would appear most presumptuous of me to suppose I could, through the printed word only, effect a change in the reader's behavior pattern. Indeed, I cannot presume to change anyone's behavior. I can change only my own. But I can let you in on how I do it so that if you are so inclined, you can change yours, too. I have faith that you have what it takes to apply successfully the ideas presented here. You will learn later why I have this simple faith.

Typical Self-Defeating Behaviors (SDBs). Some self-defeating behaviors (SDBs) that have been eliminated by others include the following:

inferiority feelings	fear of people
compulsive eating	perfectionism
procrastination	depression

bad study habits	fear of failure
withdrawal	fear of close relationships
sexual deviancy	fear of marriage

You can see from these examples that the term "self-defeating behavior" includes (a) internal feelings and attitudes, (b) recurring thoughts, and (c) outward behaviors. (A more complete list is provided in Step One.)

This may be one of the most interesting and helpful programs in which you will ever participate. The entire focus of the experience is to help you change a behavior that has been defeating to you. You may say, "What! Change *my* behavior! On no you don't! I'm returning this right now if that's what you're up to. No one is going to change *my* behavior! I bought this book to learn how to change somebody *else's* behavior, not mine!"

You are right on both counts. No one is going to change your behavior; you are totally in charge of that. And if you bought this book to learn how to change others' behaviors, you can do that, too. One of the most effective ways to change the way others react to you is to behave differently yourself.

"But ... changing *my* behavior ... that scares me!" Right again. For most of us, it is normal to feel anxiety about changing or eliminating a behavior we have had for a period of time—a behavior that has been creating adverse consequences for ourselves. These are normal feelings. But this book is designed to take you step by step through information and procedures you can apply in your personal life. Thousands have done so already. This is your chance to eliminate that bad habit, that depressed feeling, that defeating way of responding to those around you.

Already you have shown considerable courage, determination, and commitment by reading about this program. It won't all be easy, but it will be interesting and exciting. Let me repeat, it is extremely important that you follow carefully the directions in each step. If you do, you will gain the victory almost in spite of yourself.

In Step One you will be asked to choose only one behavior you want or need to eliminate. It can be one you frequently do through thinking or feeling. For example, one young mother chose to eliminate compulsive thoughts she held about hurting others. Another person chose to eliminate disturbing and unwanted sexual thoughts. Others chose to eliminate thoughts of hatred or prejudice that affected their social lives. Feelings of inferiority or depression or loneliness, or feeling dumb or nervous are some examples of "feeling" kinds of SDBs that have been eliminated. Some examples of SDBs more often considered as outward behaviors might include masturbation, procrastination, compulsive eating, homosexuality, smoking, stuttering, temper tantrums, disorganization, and biting fingernails. In this program all of the above, whether feeling, thinking, or doing, will be considered "behaviors," and in this case "self-defeating behaviors."

At this point it would be wise to get a calendar and plan ahead. Write out the date you plan to have completed each of the seven steps. This schedule will help you keep going. Our research on scheduling indicates that the best schedule for this program is to do one step of the program every five to six days until all seven steps are completed. However, variations in this schedule are permissible and sometimes necessary. It will be up to you to get all you can out of the experience. You may feel tempted to put off completing the program or to skim lightly over it because someone will not be checking up on you each step of the way. Don't let yourself do this. Great rewards will come to you from adhering to this program. It can be as deeply meaningful or as shallow as you wish to make it. It is designed in such a way that you can receive maximum benefit only by doing each step in the order in which it is presented. If you skip to the last step to find out how it ends, you will only find "the butler did it." But you will also find *you* were the butler! Don't "kill it" for yourself in that way.

Workshops to help eliminate self-defeating behaviors were based on original ideas developed by Dr. Milton R. Cudney. (note 16; 1975 A, B; 1976.) The basic ideas in this book are Dr. Cudney's, and with his permission I have revised and enlarged certain concepts, based on my own practice and experience with participants and clients over the past few years. I have taken the ideas originally designed for presentation in a group setting and designed them to be used individually and without the help of a professional counselor, psychologist, or trained group leader. However, if professional help is needed, the reader should not hesitate to seek it from competent and licensed professionals. Several clients under treatment by their psychiatrists have found it helpful to share this program with their psychiatrists to deepen the value of it as therapy. While this is a relatively new method, it has gained ready acceptance by professional people as a helpful tool in understanding and controlling human behavior.

As you can see from the limited bibliography, not much has been published on this method. However, from research on the results of its use and reports from other professionals using the program, I can say with confidence that the steps you are about to take will make a difference in your life.

The basic premise upon which the success of this method and its program is based is that as human beings we are born with great potential for creative, successful living. We already have within us a built-in striving for excellence, achievement, knowledge, and happiness. We must undergo a great deal of erroneous and negative learning to render this striving useless in our lives so that we are *not* happy when we achieve or so that we stop trying to achieve altogether.

Although the attainment of perfection toward which we naturally strive is a lifelong process, we can begin now by changing those patterns of behavior that keep us from being our best selves in moments of living and that therefore defeat us in our natural striving to be successful. How to make these behavior changes is often a difficult problem. For many, the task seems too formidable to start. By the time we are old enough to know that we have a problem, we have already become somewhat entrenched in ways of thinking and doing that created and help to maintain that problem. Unfortunately, being told to stop a habit or even determining deep within to stop it does not always help us stop.

This program was written to help *you* learn how to stop a self-defeating behavior regardless of its duration in your life.

How the self-defeating behavior started. Perhaps I could have you help me demonstrate how self-defeating behaviors originate and how you maintain them to your own disadvantage. I would like you to hold in your hands a wastepaper basket or a bucket of some kind—even a garbage can will do. I will assume, then, that you are sitting (or standing), holding in both hands a wastepaper basket or a reasonable likeness of one. I want you to imagine with me for a moment that you are about four years old and that your mother has asked you to empty the wastebasket. You have just taken it out of the house and emptied it into the large trash barrel in the back alley. Let's suppose also that it is winter; it has been snowing, and there are some boys older than you out there near the alley, throwing snowballs. Imagine they decide to throw snowballs at you in an effort to hit you. What will you do with the empty wastebasket? You might choose from several alternatives. You may choose to drop it and run or to carry it and run back into the house. Or you may choose to put it down and throw snowballs back. Or you may choose to put it over your head for protection. Or perhaps you choose to hold it in front of you so that the snowballs hit the basket rather than you. Let's suppose for the sake of this illustration you get the idea to hold it as a shield in front of you so the snowballs hit the basket rather than you—and that it feels pretty good inside you not to get hit by those snowballs. In that situation it was the most logical thing to do to avoid the hurt you might have experienced.

Now, I want you to imagine that it is six months later. It is summer, and you have been carrying that wastebasket around with you every minute since that experience last winter. In fact, you have taken it to bed with you; you have bathed with it, you have eaten with it, you have taken it outside to play; you have even gone to the movies with it. Every time you try to walk off without it, an unpleasant feeling comes from deep inside you, and you think, "What if someone saved up a snowball in the deep freeze? They'll get me right in the face with it if I don't have my wastebasket to stop it." That feeling and these thoughts keep you hanging onto the wastebasket for security. The thought of being without it makes you feel uncomfortable, perhaps insecure, even anxious. Years roll by, and here you are, still hanging onto your wastebasket. At the same time you are growing tired of it and wishing you could let it go—not have to bother with it anymore. But you have grown so accustomed to having it around that you feel it is part of you, part of your very personality, or who you really are. You have given yourself current, up-to-date and logical reasons why you keep it. But as you look at it objectively, you see it is not part of you. It is a burden that hinders you from doing many things you could do without it. It also takes energy to carry it—energy you could use for creative and constructive purposes.

You may put the basket down now; and thank you for helping me.

Your self-defeating behavior is like that wastebasket. You started it in a moment of stress, fear, anxiety, anger, or even pleasure— when just being yourself did not seem to be enough. You had to take on additional behaviors such as attitudes or ways of thinking or outward actions in order to cope with that situation. Whatever you did worked for that or a similar situation. But then you became somewhat fearful of giving it up, so you continued to use it. At times, even when you were quite determined never to do it again, you found yourself doing it anyway. In this program, we are going to separate that behavior from what you *are* so that you can see it

9

is not you but what you *do* that is the problem. You are the sole doer, or it would not get done. You choose to do it. Even though you have suffered many adverse consequences from doing it, you have built up a rationale or set of reasons that help you maintain the habit.

You may think that once you have identified your SDB and how you do it, you would naturally stop doing it. It doesn't work that way. Suppose that if, after you had held onto that wastebasket for several years, I came along and said, "I'm going to take that away from you." What would your reaction be? Usually it is something like this: "Oh no you're not! I'm going to hang onto it. I need it!" We must recognize that there is this feeling of "need" for the SDB involved in the process of retaining it. Otherwise, you would have given it up long ago, and it would not be a concern at this moment in your life. The fact is that you have maintained it up to now.

You also need to recognize that people use certain normal behaviors in an attempt to hang on to the very behavior they want to let go. We call these behaviors "defeating-the-program behaviors." You'll find a list of such behaviors later on. It is most important that you let yourself become aware of all such behaviors you are using. Be as honest and self-observant as you can so that you will not defeat the purpose for your following this program.

You will be required to choose one behavior and to keep a daily diary regarding your thoughts, feelings, actions, and struggles that are in some way related to the behavior you are trying to change. You will include in the diary the efforts you make to apply the principles presented to you in each step. The more specific you are in describing *what* you do and *how* you do it, the better you will see what you are doing to keep this behavior pattern going. But be brief. Avoid telling *why* you keep this behavior. *Why* usually takes you into the past. Hanging onto the past may become an excuse or a reason for continuing the behavior in the present. In this way you may defeat yourself. There is only one point in the program at which the reasons "why" are discussed. Whatever reasons you might have given yourself as to why you continue the behavior will not help stop it. Rather, they will serve as ways of helping to keep the self-defeating behavior going, as you will see. In your diary focus on exactly *what* you do and *how* you do it.

Many people have found the diary to be one of the most important and beneficial parts of this program. In it you can write your innermost experiences, thoughts, and concerns. Through this method you allow yourself to see more clearly what is going on inside you.

It will help you get in touch with yourself—help you describe what deep human struggles you are having in letting the person that is *you* come out from behind the self-defeating behavior.

Write a paragraph or a page each day describing these feelings, thoughts, and actions. Later in the program I will give you a method to help you analyze what you have written so that you may be able to see yourself in a new light. You need to know, as best you can, exactly what is happening inside you as you go through the program so that you can do a good job of getting a "handle" on your SDB.

Your diary may be kept confidential while you are working on this program, but later you may desire to share it with someone you love and trust. The more you write, the more it will help you. When people write their problems, fears, and feelings or describe in written detail their own behaviors, they are doubly helped: first, because they become more acutely aware of what they are doing and can begin to see some solutions; and second, because they have something tangible outside themselves upon which to look back from time to time to see progress as they grow out of an old pattern. Many great people keep a personal diary. You can begin today to write yours.

Here is an example of a typical diary entry (the SDB was procrastination): Saturday, Feb. _____ "The day was a good one—for my SDB. My SDB happened again. I was supposed to get my room cleaned up, and I planned to study at least three hours to get my term paper done. What happened is that my friend came over early to see if I would go skiing. He was so excited about it that we went and had a ball until we were both so tired we sat in the car and slept until after dark. When we finally got back and ate, it was late and I was dead tired. I said to myself, 'tomorrow' when I looked at my term paper. I have good intentions, but when the chips are down I can't seem to say 'no,' and I give in, even when I know how bad the consequences will be." (Composite Diary.)

In addition to the daily diary sheets, summary forms are shown for each step. Spaces on these forms are for listing relevant information regarding your SDB as it pertains to each step of the program. It is important that you complete these forms to the best of your ability and precisely as instructed. Remember: complete only one step at a time on *one* SDB. You are now ready for Step One.

Reference Notes:

1. Chamberlain, Jonathan M., and Heaps, Richard A.
1974 Self-Control Training for Eliminating Self-Defeating Behaviors. Pa-

per presented at the Utah Personnel and Guidance Association Annual Conference, Salt Lake City, Utah (April).

2. Chamberlain, Jonathan M.
   1977 A Workshop That Works Even If You Are Not There—Or How to Eliminate Your SDBs by Mail. Unpublished paper presented at "ESDB Update 77," Grand Rapids, Michigan (May).

3. Chamberlain, Jonathan M.
   1975 A Proposal—Eliminating a Family-Defeating Behavior: A Short-term Family Therapy Workshop Using the ESDB Model in Family Psychotherapy. Paper presented at the conference of the Utah Association of Marriage and Family Counselors, Salt Lake City, Utah (January).

4. Chamberlain, Jonathan M.
   1975 The Workshop on Eliminating Self-Defeating Behaviors: An Individualized Group Technique. Paper presented at the Sweetwater County Mental Health Association, Rock Springs, Wyoming (April).

5. Bills, Conrad C.
   1973 Effects of an Eliminating Self-Defeating Behavior Workshop on Self-Concept and Behavior of Elementary School Students. Unpublished master's thesis, Brigham Young University, Provo, Utah.

6. Bohn, Robert F.
   1975 Effects of the Eliminating Self-Defeating Behavior Workshop with and without the Daily Diary. Unpublished doctoral dissertation, Brigham Young University, Provo, Utah.

7. Coombs, David H.
   1974 The Elimination of Self-Defeating Behaviors and Their Relationships to Self-Concept. Unpublished doctoral dissertation, Brigham Young University, Provo, Utah.

8. Fiester, F. L.
   1972 An Investigation of the Process and Outcomes of the Elimination of Self-Defeating Behavior Workshop: A Group Treatment for Specific College Student Problems. Kalamazoo, Michigan: Michigan State University, 73-5371.

9. Forsyth, Robert D.
   1976 A Comparison of Change in Locus of Control for Massed and Spaced Eliminating Self-Defeating Behavior Workshops. Unpublished doctoral dissertation, Brigham Young University, Provo, Utah.

10. Hendricks, J. Vance
    1972 The Elimination of Self-Defeating Behaviors and Their Relationship to Study Effectiveness, Self-Concept, and Anxiety. Unpub-

lished doctoral dissertation, Brigham Young University, Provo, Utah.

11. Jacobs, Alvin W.
   1974 The Effects of Hand Holding in the Guided Imagery Phase of the Eliminating Self-Defeating Behavior Workshop. Unpublished doctoral dissertation, Brigham Young University, Provo, Utah.

12. Johnson, E. Kim
   1975 The Treatment of Smoking as a Self-Defeating Behavior and Prediction of Behavior Change and Maintenance. Unpublished doctoral dissertation, Brigham Young University, Provo, Utah.

13. Parks, Cristen R.
   1976 Factors Affecting Performance in the Workshops for Elimination of Self-Defeating Behaviors. Unpublished doctoral dissertation, Brigham Young University, Provo, Utah.

14. Seamons, T. R., Heaps, R. A., and Chamberlain, J. M.
   1973 Techniques for Eliminating Self-Defeating Behaviors. Paper presented at the American Personnel and Guidance Association Convention, San Diego, California (February).

15. Stampfl, T. G.
   1961 Implosive Therapy, a Learning Theory Derived from Psychodynamic Therapeutic Technique. Paper presented at the University of Illinois, Urbana, Ill.

16. Cudney, Milton R.
   1971 Elimination of Self-Defeating Behavior. Unpublished paper, Western Michigan University, Kalaamazoo, Michigan.

References:

Berne, Eric
   1961 Transactional Analysis in Psychotherapy. New York: Grove Press.

Brigham Young University Bulletin
   1977 Home Study Catalogue of Courses, Brigham Young University, Provo, Utah, pp. 35, 152.

Chamberlain, Jonathan M.
   1973 Eliminating Self-Defeating Behaviors. In A. Mitchell and C. D. Johnson (Eds.), Therapeutic Techniques: working models for the helping professional. Fullerton, Calif.: California Personnel and Guidance Association.

Chamberlain, Jonathan M.
   1976 Eliminating a Self-Defeating Behavior. Handbook for Education 514Rx-1, a Brigham Young University Home Study Course: How

to Eliminate a Self-Defeating Behavior, Fourth edition, Brigham Young University Printing Services, Provo, Utah.

Chamberlain, Jonathan M.
1977 Treatment of Self-Defeating Behaviors, chapter 5 in Gloria G. Harris (Ed.). The Group Treatment of Human Problems: A Social Learning Approach. New York: Grune & Stratton, Inc.

Cudney, Milton R.
1975A Eliminating Self-Defeating Behaviors. Kalamazoo, Michigan: Life Giving Enterprises.

Cudney, Milton R.
1975B Self-Defeating Characters. Kalamazoo, Michigan: Life Giving Enterprises.

Cudney, Milton R.
1976 Implementation and Innovation of the Elimination of Self-Defeating Behavior Theory. Kalamazoo, Michigan: Life Giving Enterprises.

Ellis, Albert
1973 Rational Emotive Therapy in Current Psychotherapies. In R. Corsini (Ed.), Itasca, Illinois: Peacock Publishers.

Glasser, William
1965 Reality Therapy: A New Approach to Psychiatry. New York: Harper and Row.

Krumboltz, John D., and Thoresen, Carl E.
1969 Behavioral Counseling: Cases and Techniques. New York: Holt, Rinehart & Winston.

Maslow, Abraham
1968 Toward a Psychology of Being, Second edition. Princeton, New Jersey: D. Van Nostrand Co.

Moody, Raymond A., Jr.
1976 Life After Life. New York: Bantam Books.

Parks, C. R., Becker, M., Chamberlain, J. M., and Crandall, J. M.
1975 "Eliminating a Self-Defeating Behavior and Change in Locus of Control." Journal of Psychology, 91 (September): 115–30.

Perls, Fritz
1969 Gestalt Therapy Verbations. Toronto: Bantam Books.

Piaget, B. W., and Lazarus, A. A.
1961 "The Use of Rehearsal-Desensitization." Psychotherapy: Theory, Research and Practice, 6: 265–66.

Rogers, Carl R.
1961 On Becoming a Person. Boston: Houghton Mifflin.

Wolpe, Joseph, and Lazarus, A. A.
1966 Behavior Therapy Techniques. New York: Pergamon Press.

STEP ONE:
HOW DO I DO
MY SELF-DEFEATING
BEHAVIOR?

YOUR OBJECTIVES FOR STEP ONE

You will be able to:

1. Determine *one* self-defeating behavior (SDB) to eliminate.
2. Keep a simple diary of your thoughts, feelings, and actions regarding that SDB.
3. Make a list of the ways you do this SDB.
4. Catch yourself doing, or about to do, your SDB and describe your thoughts, feelings, and actions either in your diary or on the summary form.

HOW TO PROCEED

In order to achieve these objectives, you must complete the following activities:

1. Read "How Do I Do My SDB?" "Which One Will I Choose?" and "Defeating the Change Program," following this list.
2. After you have kept your daily diary for at least four days and have filled in the summary form for Step One, read "My Critique for Step One." Critique your writings.
3. When you have completed all of the above, you may go on to Step Two.

How Do I Do My SDB?

As you carry out your SDB, you are your own worst enemy. You are altogether, all the way, completely, the doer of your self-defeating behavior. It is impossible for you to carry an SDB from one moment in your life to a future moment without your actively doing it. You make it happen. You are responsible for its continuation, whether you want that responsibility or not. As the cartoon character Pogo said, "We have met the enemy, and it is us."

When you really understand this concept at a deep level, you will drop your SDB. A self-defeating behavior is not something you *are*, but something you *do*. It is a behavior you learned at a time of conflict, stress, anxiety, fear, loneliness, boredom, or hostility, when reacting naturally didn't bring satisfactory results in relieving yourself of unpleasant feelings.

The SDB, then, is simply a way of coping with your present world—a way of responding or acting that is only partly, or not at all, effective now and therefore is a hindrance to better responses and a more complete life. Consequently, your SDB is not a condition or a sickness; rather, it is a behavior. Remember that you were not born with it, and so it is something you learned to do.

Life continues to offer you new moments of living. These moments can be filled with either self-defeating or creative actions. If you desire the creative route, you must begin by completing each of the activities that follow.

Which One Will I Choose?

Now, the first thing to do is to choose a self-defeating behavior that you want to eliminate. If you have not already chosen one, the list below may be of help. You may find it helpful to read down this list and check all those that apply to you, then go back over those you have checked and double check the ones that create the most problems for you *now*. Those you have checked will be somewhat related to each other. Try to choose one that seems more at the root of (or to be the cause of) the others you have checked. Examples of behaviors the program can help you eliminate (Adapted from Cudney, note 1):

Inferiority feelings
Fear of groups
Racial prejudice
Lack of motivation
Homosexuality
Compulsive eating
Feelings of hatred
Alienation of others
Depression
Fear of the unknown

Inability to concentrate
Unrealistic distrust of others
Fear of stating your point of view
Procrastination
Difficulty in decision making
Perfectionism
Withdrawal
Voyeurism (peeping tom)
Compulsive lying

18

Compulsive thoughts
Alcoholism
Feelings of meaninglessness
Stuttering
Fear of hurting others
Folding up under pressure when challenged
Temper
Negativism
Fear of failure
Underachievement
Dependency
Excessive overweight
Masturbation
Compulsive sexual behavior
Boredom
Excessive worry
Psychosomatic illnesses
Feelings of loneliness
Drug abuse
Excessive guilt
Defensiveness
Fear of expressing deep feelings
Inability to say "No"
To know what you want to say but unable to get the right words out
Wasting time
Forgetfulness
Always feeling pushed by someone

Fear of getting close to the opposite sex
Fear of commitment
Fear of taking a test
Excessive attempts to please others
Quitting in the middle of difficult tasks
Authority problems
Disorganization
Poor planning
Wait until last minute to do things
Fear of God
Lack of confidence in yourself
Fear of rejection
Fear of death
Excessive daydreaming
Unhappiness by yourself
Insomnia
Never on time
Can't find needed things
Fear of being yourself
Unrealistic expectations of self and others
Unforgiving of self
Extreme nervousness
Avoidance of responsibility
Inability to give yourself in a loving relationship

Choose only one SDB on which to focus during the entire program. Feel free to choose a thought, feeling, or action without which your life would be happier, whether the behavior is on the above list or not. This is merely a list of possibilities, suggested by others. In choosing the SDB you would like to eliminate, consider one that causes problems not only for you but perhaps also for others around you. However, if you should choose one that only *others* want you to change, you might not invest the time, thought, and energy necessary to apply the principles in this program; thus you will make no change at all and will defeat the program. The one you choose should be your own private choice. For now, only you need know what it is. However, it may be to your advantage, later on, for you to discuss your SDB with a trusted friend, religious leader, or professional helping person. This choice is up to you.

If you choose an SDB that is so "safe" that it will not make any difference in your life whether you eliminate it or not, you will have missed an opportunity to work on something meaningful to you, and you will likely not commit yourself to eliminate it.

Many people are concerned that they choose the "right" one to work on. They feel they have several others that should be dealt with at the same time. They ask, "Can't I work on more than one at the same time?—I have several. In fact, that's my list [referring to the list of suggested SDBs]." The answer is that if you try to work on more than one during this experience, it may turn out to be a good way to defeat the program and to be a method for hanging on to the behavior you say you are trying to eliminate. Working on one self-defeating behavior during this experience is almost a full-time job. After completing the program, you may begin working on another behavior, using the information and the skills you will have mastered by then to help you.

If, after you begin to work on your SDB, you come to feel that your first choice is only a symptom of a deeper one, and you want to change to the deeper one, that will be permissible.

Most of our self-defeating behaviors are interrelated, so that when we work on eliminating one that is at the heart of the problem, the other behaviors supported by that one will be dropped more easily as well.

I have observed, as I mentioned in the introduction, that everyone seems to have one or more self-defeating behaviors. A side effect of this experience will be your awareness that others around you are behaving as they do partly because of their own SDBs.

If you are currently in treatment for emotional problems with a qualified psychologist, psychiatrist, or counselor, you should continue treatment and share with that person your experience in this program. You may find such a person especially helpful when you do Step Seven.

When you have decided on the SDB you want to eliminate, write the one you have chosen on the appropriate lines on the Summary Form for Step One. Stop here until you have done this. It is important to write the SDB because it is so easy to "forget" what it is you are working on.

Now, brainstorm with yourself and list on the lower part of the summary form for Step One exactly how you do your SDB. Doing this will help you find out your feelings, thoughts, and physical actions that trigger your SDB. Some examples may help:

1. A participant working to eliminate excess weight listed thirty-five ways she got food into her mouth, the way she stirred it, where she did most of her eating, at what times she ate, how she felt, and her thoughts as she ate.

2. Another participant working to drop his SDB of feeling socially inadequate listed the thoughts, feelings, and circumstances he used to "do" his feelings of social inadequacy. For one he wrote: "I convince myself (by certain thoughts and feelings) that if I don't impress certain key people (anyone whom I decide to impress), I'm just not very adequate." This is just one way he did his SDB. (Cudney, Note 1.)

3. Another participant working on his fear of marriage listed: "I make myself feel very inadequate in my ability to hold a job and to just cope with life's daily problems. I tell myself I couldn't bear to have my wife better adjusted than myself ... and at the same time I couldn't bear to have her worse off than I feel, either .... I am drawn to the most attractive girls who are not attracted to me, and I get hurt. When I do find someone who really accepts me, I then say to myself, 'There must be something wrong with her if she accepts me.' I keep girls at a distance so I don't have to risk much. I give the impression that I'm playing the field." (Composite entry.)

4. A participant working on eliminating depressed feelings wrote: "The slightest difficulties in the family make me want to go to my room and never come out. I notice how poorly I discipline the children and how ineffective I am at just managing the housework. I feel 'what's the use' all day long so that I tend to give up easily when things go the least bit wrong. I talk far too long on the phone while things are going to pot all around me." (Composite entry.)

Now stop here until you have listed all of the ways you can think of regarding *how* you do your SDB, *where* you do it, and *what* exactly you do. Don't worry about *why* you do it yet.

Defeating the Change Program

Although people willingly volunteer to get into this program, at some time during the program most people try to defeat it in an attempt to keep their SDB going. One way people try to defeat the program is by using the very SDB they came into the program to change. For example, if you choose procrastination as your SDB, you may try to procrastinate in this program, and thus you may defeat it so that you can continue to procrastinate as before. If you use inferiority feelings, you will probably attempt to create inferior feelings while doing your homework assignments and your diary and will not want to face these feelings so that you can defeat the program and keep your SDB. If you depress yourself often, you could do that while taking this program and thus use the feeling you created to help you defeat the program so that you can keep the behavior going. If you use blaming as a means to keep your SDB, you could blame the author, the program, or those around you to keep you from doing the program effectively.

During the program, you will be given ample opportunity to see how you are trying to defeat it. It will help you if you will be open about it, for not being open about how you may be trying to defeat the program is a way of defeating it. By getting your methods of trying to defeat the program out in the open, you will have a chance to see your behavior in a new light and to receive information about it that you didn't have before; and this will help you be less defeating.

Following is a partial list of ways former participants have tried to defeat themselves in the program. (Cudney, note 1.) I share the list with you in the hope that it will help you eliminate your self-defeating behavior. Read through the list and check those you may be tempted to use, then try not to use them. (Read the list over again later to determine if you are using some new ones by then.)

- **To withhold important information from the program that is necessary to bring about change. (For example, not being specific in your diary.)**
- **To put responsibility for change entirely on others. (*They* have to change; then I will.)**
- **To be noncommital to the change program. (I'll give it a half-hearted try.)**
- **Not to fulfill the assignments given.**
- **When something that has to be done in order to effect change becomes very clear, not to go ahead and do it.**
- **To use various means of defeating the change program as a way of feeling legitimate about getting discouraged and giving up.**
- **To avoid anxiety-laden data within yourself; to avoid risk.**
- **To maintain an attitude that change is impossible.**
- **To believe that something worse will happen if the SDB is given up.**

22

- To "forget" partway through the program the SDB you are trying to change.
- To write about various subjects in your diary that may be of real interest but are irrelevant to the change process.
- To convince yourself that this program demands you assume too much responsibility for your own behavior, and you don't want to behave so responsibly.
- To have been involved in a change program in the past, to have defeated that one, and then to use that as an excuse not to do what it takes to bring about a change in this program.
- To approach the program with the idea that these principles will be applied later, and thus do nothing now to change.
- To focus on *why* the behavior is kept going rather than *how* it is kept going. (Do not concern yourself at all regarding *why* at this point.)
- To imagine that the time taken to change will inconvenience others or yourself too much. (If I change, it will shake them up too much.)
- To write down ideas that are important, then not do anything about them.
- To eat or doodle as a way of distracting yourself from getting information that will help you let the SDB go.
- To get sleepy in this change program and not to own up to how the sleepiness was created. (Being sleepy serves the purpose of closing you off to ideas that will bring change.)
- To focus on another person as a way of avoiding yourself. (I'll change him or her.)
- To go into a trance to keep the behavior if all your past ways of keeping the SDB don't work.
- To make honest progress, to feel better, and then to drop out of the program before full change occurs. (Watch out for this one. Don't be a drop-out.)
- To avoid being responsible for a behavior by maintaining that supernatural forces are responsible, then thinking the SDB is beyond your control.
- If you believe in prayer, to pray for divine assistance to help change the SDB, then not do anything to help yourself.
- To work hard at understanding one step in the program such as the "prices" paid in Step Three or the "techniques" used in Step five, but not allow yourself clear understanding of another concept such as the "inner choices" in Step Four.

- When a friend uses a technique to keep an SDB going, to support that person in doing it with the hope that the friend will support your SDB later on.
- To get close to anxiety feelings and then to make them unreal so that you can scare yourself with them.
- To identify specific things that need to be done to change, but not to do anything, telling yourself that all the angles regarding the behavior have not been explored yet.
- To keep yourself as an observer of the program rather than as a full participant.
- When you have something important to say, to keep it to yourself.
- To take on all sorts of other new tasks while in this program as a way of not having to concentrate on letting the behavior go, and so you can claim that you are just too busy to do it now.
- To make the program a frightening experience in your mind in order to scare you out of continuing to the conclusion.
- To believe that your SDB is much more severe than everyone else's and to use this to justify hanging on to it.
- To convince yourself that the SDB is not severe enough to take up time or effort to change it.
- To convince yourself that you have never succeeded at anything anyway, so why break that record by trying now.
- To tell yourself that since no one else knows about your attempts to change the SDB in this program, you can easily keep it going and no one will be the wiser.
- To make yourself believe that since no one else is going to read the diary or summary forms but yourself, there is no reason to write it all down.
- To convince yourself that you need someone else to be accountable for your progress in this program, and then not find someone you can trust to help you with it.

Although you want to let your self-defeating behaviors go, please understand that for most people there is a certain amount of reluctance connected to making changes. Thus, they try to hang on to their SDB even when they are participating in a change program.

The more you try to defeat the change program, the smaller the chance you will have of achieving a full behavioral change. If you will determine now to keep doing the assigned homework and to apply the concepts taught, you will succeed in spite of yourself.

STEP ONE SUMMARY FORM: WHAT I DO AND HOW I DO IT DATE_____

The Self-Defeating Behavior I have chosen to eliminate is:

_____

_____

(Write above the specific self-defeating behavior you want to eliminate; see the "examples" list for suggestions.)

INSTRUCTIONS: On these summary forms you are to list the ideas you get with each step. List below what, when, and *how* you do your self-defeating behavior, i.e., all the ways, thoughts, feelings, and actions. Add to this list as you gain insight into additional ways. You are the world's expert on your SDB. (Remember, we are not concerned with *why* you do it at this time.)

_____
_____
_____
_____
_____
_____
_____
_____
_____
_____
_____
_____
_____
_____
_____
_____
_____
_____
_____
_____
_____

(Use additional paper if needed)

Critique for Step One

Before going to Step Two, let me share with you how you can gain some additional insight from the writing you have done thus far. By now you should have written in your diary for at least four days and completed the list on the summary form for Step One as you were instructed to do. What I am about to show you will have little meaning if you have not done this.

Critiquing Your Summary Form

Look at your summary form for Step One. Wherever you can in the statements in which you describe your SDB—what you do and how you do it—add one or more of the following phrases: "I decide to" or "I decided to" or "I tell myself" or "I make myself feel" or "I choose to." Here are some examples.

Example 1. This example is from a person with the SDB of compulsive eating.

Before this Exercise

I eat when I come into the house.

I grab something to eat whenever I go somewhere.

I eat more than I can comfortably hold.

I get my husband to invite me out to dinner.

I feel I have to eat all that's on my plate.

I hate to waste food.

I nibble while I'm fixing dinner.

I eat leftovers from the plates of others when cleaning up dinner.

After this Exercise

I *decide to* eat when I come into the house.

I *decide to* grab something to eat whenever I go somewhere

I *choose to* eat more than I can comfortably hold.

I *decide to* get my husband to invite me out to dinner.

I *make myself* feel I have to eat all that's on my plate

I *tell myself I* hate to waste food.

I *choose to* nibble while I'm fixing dinner.

I *decide to* eat leftovers from the plates of others when cleaning up dinner.

Example 2: The SDB described below is an example of compulsive sexual thinking. (Composite examples.)

26

Before this Exercise	After this Exercise
Girls' short skirts get me excited.	I let girls' short skirts get me excited.
I get turned on in my mind when I see girls in tight sweaters.	*decide to* I / get turned on in my mind when I see girls in tight sweaters.
I feel turned on when I see girls in low-cut dresses.	*make myself* I / feel turned on when I see girls in low-cut dresses.
Some T.V. shows and pictures get me excited.	*I make or let* / Some T.V. shows and pictures get me excited.
When I try to study, my mind wanders.	*I decide to let* When I try to study, / my mind wanders/.

Example 3: The SDB described below is an example of excessive worry.

Before this Exercise	After this Exercise
I worry about the world situation.	*choose to* I / worry about the world situation.
I can't sleep at night so I think about all the things that went wrong in my life.	*don't* *can choose to* I ~~can't~~ sleep at night so I / think about all the things that went wrong in my life.
I'm afraid of what the future will bring.	*make myself feel* I'm / afraid of what the future will bring.
I think back on all my mistakes.	I think back on all my mistakes.
I can't stop thinking all night until morning.	*decide to not sleep by thinking negative thoughts* I / ~~can't stop thinking~~ all night until morning.

With these few examples from others, you should be able to revise your own writings. Adding these phrases is meant to help you begin to think differently about how you *decide* or *choose* to do your SDB, and to help you become more aware of your part in doing it. When you think of it, how can your SDB occur again unless you *decide* to allow it to? We will discuss in more detail later how and when we make these decisions.

As you continue in this experience, you should come to learn also that you are in charge of your feelings, moods, and attitudes as well as your thoughts. You will learn that even when you are seemingly out of control, you are really still in control.

Critiquing Your Diary

Now you are ready to go back over your diary entries and critique them in a similar way by writing in statements that will force you to consider in a new and perhaps more objective manner what you have written. Try to look at your diary statements through the eyes of an objective person who now insists that you assume the responsibility for doing your SDB and who does not take kindly to many of the usual excuses offered for doing it. Try to point out in writing how the author of the diary is trying to disown responsibility by shifting the blame for choosing to do the SDB to others or to circumstances. Be frank and honest but not brutal or unkind.

Perhaps an example would help you at this point. The following is an example of a diary entry with an objective critique at the right.

DAILY DIARY (Composite diary.)   My Critique

SDB   Compulsive Eating   Date Jan 1

I chose to wait until this new year began to get started so I could do my thing first and then make a resolution. I decided to commit myself to take charge over what I eat.

The first day of a New Year. Wow! Am I ever full of nice resolutions about my diet and how thin I am going to be someday when I take control of this SDB.

I carefully avoided plans to take charge over the moments coming next but instead looked way ahead at the year—"someday." I could choose to start now, in this moment, then "someday" will be taken care of.

I made a resolution the first thing this morning that I was going to eat sensibly all year long and take only moderate servings of the foods I am allowed to eat. No more gorging for me when others are not around

I am determined to change my pattern of behavior!

28

as I have been doing! And no cheating on myself. After all, I am wise enough to know I'm only cheating myself—and nobody else.

I made all these resolutions in my head before I left the bedroom. But when I walked into the front room, there was this delicious array of my most tempting chocolate creams and fruitcake left from the neighborhood party we had last night.

True! Who am I trying to kid by doing my SDB?

I decided not to write them down because that would be too binding on me.

Who am I kidding? I knew they were there. I left them there so I could tempt myself the next day!

What a blast. I stuffed myself until I hurt—all the while telling myself I'm starting a new leaf tomorrow. (After all, it's New Year's Eve, and what's the good of living if you can't have fun once in a while.) Well, I cleaned up the candy junk in the living room, and when I got into the kitchen, I found myself stuffing salty buttered popcorn into my mouth without even thinking what I was doing; and without a moment's hesitation I cut off a large slice of fruitcake, spread it with leftover frosting from a mixing bowl in the sink, and downed it with a glass of punch. Then I realized what I had done and felt sick and angry. "You with your big resolution," I told myself. "What kind of a glutton are you anyway? You can't even go one hour without blowing the whole thing. Oh well, January 2 is a good day to start things anyway." I felt more discouraged as the day went on. I seemed determined to finish off those chocolate creams even though I hid them so I wouldn't. But just knowing they were there bugged me; so I sneaked and ate one at a time until they were gone. Yuck!

Today I will behave irresponsibly; but "tomorrow" I will decide to behave responsibly? But I can't behave tomorrow nor take charge then—only now, in this moment.

But do my cells know the difference?

I say "found myself" as if I were not in control of what I put into me. Who is in charge of what gets inside of me? I AM! I could decide to "find myself" a few minutes earlier, before doing my SDB! I timed it just right! I decided to eat popcorn. No one made me do it.

I chose to drink the sweet punch.

Did I hide them *from* myself or *for* myself?

_____

_____

_____

___*What is wrong with me? I hate myself,*___

___*and now I feel depressed. What's the use?*___

_____

_____

_____

_____

_____

_____

Did I tell myself that something must be "wrong with me" so I can use this as a "reason" for doing my SDB, and shift *my* responsibility to something else so I can do it and get away with it?

In these ways I made myself feel depressed and discouraged—techniques used to keep my SDB going.

Try now to make similar kinds of critical remarks on your own diary entries. Do not feel that you must do a perfect job of critiquing your writings at the beginning (especially if your SDB is perfectionism). Allow yourself time to learn a few more ways of thinking about your own behavior and to develop some skill by practicing this critiquing exercise on yourself.

At this point in the program, many people complain they never realized before how much they do this SDB and how sneaky they are about keeping it going. Some complain they "find themselves" doing it even more often now that they are trying to give it up. These are normal experiences and seem related to the fact that there is in all of us the conflicting desire to hang onto the SDB at the same time we are attempting to rid ourselves of it. Thus, there is often created a two-way pull within us as we try to give it up. This may be partly due to our increased awareness that we are doing it. But mostly it is related to the fear we have of giving it up and doing without it. We will discuss this fear in a later step.

Because this program is serious and has the potential of eliminating an SDB, some people decide to go on one last "binge" before the "famine" comes. However, this kind of behavior is soon recognized as the "defeating the program" technique it really is, aimed only at helping to keep the SDB going longer. Watch out for it.

After you have gone over your summary form and your diary entries for Step One, you are ready to go on to Step Two.

Reference Notes:

1. Cudney, Milton R.
    1971 Elimination of Self-Defeating Behavior. Unpublished paper, Western Michigan University, Kalamazoo, Michigan.

STEP TWO:
HOW DO I DISOWN RESPONSIBILITY FOR DOING MY SELF-DEFEATING BEHAVIOR?

YOUR OBJECTIVES FOR STEP TWO

You will be able to:
1. Recognize and state a personal, negative label you have been living under and change it to a positive one.
2. List the ways you disown responsibility for your self-defeating behavior.

HOW TO PROCEED

In order to complete Step Two, you must do the following:
1. Read "Disowning my SDB" (following) and the information about labels and blaming. Do the requested assignments when you come to them in the reading.
2. Continue to write a daily diary of the thoughts, feelings, and actions related to your SDB.
3. After you have done the above, have completed the summary form, and have kept your diary for at least four more days, critique your writing for this step; you will be ready to go on to Step Three.

Disowning My SDB

All of us who have a SDB have ways of disowning full responsibility for what we do so that we can continue to do it. When you fully and deeply recognize not only *how* you do your SDB as in Step One but also that you are responsible for doing it in your current moments of living, you are at the threshold of behavior change. You are behaving irresponsibly whenever you do a repeated behavior that brings adverse results to you. This step in the program should help you assume more responsibility for the results you derive from life's experiences. It is normal to want beneficial results from daily living rather than hurtful ones.

Two major ways of disowning responsibility for SDBs are (1) using negative self-labels, and (2) blaming external causes. We will discuss each of these in turn.

I Disown Responsibility by Using Negative Self-Labels

Living under a negative or defeating label is a technique for disowning responsibility. A part of shifting the responsibility for a SDB is the way you automatically think of yourself. Most people constantly remind themselves of certain conditions or "facts" about themselves that help to maintain the SDB. These little reminders fit the self-image that we hold of ourselves and are somewhat the same as labels we give ourselves or that others have given to us. Labels may be positive or negative, depending on their effects on our lives. The labels that are closely tied to our SDBs are negative ones.

As we mature through early childhood we learn from those significant persons around us what *they* think we are. In these important formative years we form our self-images. We catch glimpses of ourselves in the "mirrors" others present to us, and we believe those images of ourselves. However, to the extent those mirrors are warped because of the SDBs and imperfections of those people, to that extent our own self-image may be distorted and untrue. By this means we form and come to adopt an erroneous self-image. We then carry this self-image around with us as a label because we do not know anything better to believe about ourselves. If those mirrors presented to us are severely warped, like the mirrors in an amusement park our self-image will likely be distorted and erroneous. Not knowing any better, we set about to uphold—through our SDBs—whatever image of ourselves we have formed, hurting our real selves.

It is a strange thing that what you continually tell yourself deep down has a tendency to become a self-fulfilling prophecy. The statement "For as he thinketh in his heart, so is he" (Proverbs 23:7) is a true saying. But you can consciously and purposefully change what you "think in your heart," or what you tell yourself about yourself. This change in thinking and in verbal self-references can bring about a change in the outcome of your behavior (Felker, 1974: 35,36).

Changing your old label to a new label can be done in two ways. There is a great difference, for example, between saying to your-

32

self—or living under the label—"I am a liar" and a similar label, "I *do* lying." In the first label, the "I am" idea seems very permanent and long-lasting and all-inclusive. It seems to mean that you continually lie every day, all week long, all year long. It does not leave room for the idea that on many occasions you tell the truth. This "I am" idea also carries with it the feeling that it is an inherited condition that will not or cannot be changed. There is in it, further, a certain resignation that it will always be so or that it is part of you, rather than a behavior you learned to do and can stop doing.

On the other hand, an "I do" label, while still being negative, seems to connote the feeling that there is a possibility for change, because it describes a behavior rather than a person. It seems to carry the idea of occasional rather than continuous occurrences of the behavior, and it leaves open more freedom to improve.

You can change negative labels from an "I am" connotation to an "I do" connotation very easily.

Another way to change a negative label to a positive one is by simply stating the opposite of the negative one. For example: "I am nonathletic" is a negative statement that could be changed to "I am athletic." Other examples might be "I am fat" to "I am thin," "I am a compulsive eater" to "I am in control over what I eat," or "I eat sensibly."

As simple as these few words may be, I cannot stress enough the shaping power they have in your life. This can be tested out by purposefully switching your own negative or self-defeating label to a positive one and reminding yourself of it often for at least two weeks. You can do this in either of the two ways described above, but the more positive the label is stated, the better, even if it does not seem "right" to say it at first.

Other examples of labels that have been shifted to a more helpful behavioral direction are: "I do a fat-making behavior," "I do compulsive eating," "I do an inferiority feeling," "I do a fear," "I do a depression."

By becoming more aware of your thoughts and actions you can be in control of what you think. You can make certain that your thoughts are positive and self-enhancing through your own decision to make them so. By this means you can begin to gain control over your feelings and actions.

I Can Experiment with My New Positive Label

On the summary form for Step Two, write a negative label under which you have been living for some time that is either closely related to the SDB or is the same as the SDB. Then change that label in one or both of the ways described above. Write your changes on the same form. Finally, remind yourself of the new label as often as you can for two or more weeks. Having it printed on a small card to keep in your pocket or purse or on the mirror in the bathroom as well as in your pocket or purse may help. Say it out loud often, several times daily. Many have found it helpful to change their wristwatch to the other wrist as a reminder to say their new label. You might choose a specific color, and every time you see that color, say your new label. Or you might put a button or a bean in your shoe to remind you to say it often. Do this for about a week.

Don't concern yourself that it may sound totally false at first. Give yourself time to believe it and to let the positive power of it work in your life.

You can experiment with yourself in regard to positive labels and allow yourself to desire to believe that they can be true. Let this desire work in you until you can make room for personal growth. It may help to compare your positive label to a seed. In order for a seed to germinate, two basic conditions must be present: wetness and warmth. When these two conditions are met long enough—for several days—the seed can begin to swell and to sprout. You can provide the conditions needed to help your new positive label sprout and take root by giving the label much *thought* and *action*. These are the wetness and warmth.

Self-referent thoughts are also like seeds in that they can produce only more of their own kind: positive thoughts can produce only more of the same, plus positive feelings and actions. The same principle is true of negative thoughts in their negative results. You are in charge of which thoughts yours will be, either positive or negative. In this way you are also in charge of the results you get—the fruits of the plant you have nurtured.

What happens when you neglect to give your new label sufficient thought and action? Like any seed, it will not take root and will not bear fruit. You must nourish the words of your positive label by first thinking and then acting on them, looking forward to positive results, not backward to past mistakes and failures. Some have called this positive tree a tree of life, for it is indeed life-giving.

"While putting myself through this SDB change program a few years ago, I discovered that I could change my old negative label by thinking 'I am athletic.' At first it seemed to be a ridiculous thing to tell myself because I obviously was not. But I enrolled in a physical fitness program for university faculty members. When I went to the first meeting and learned what was required, I immediately began to figure out ways to defeat the program. I told myself such things as 'You know your heart won't take peddling an Urgocycle every morning for an hour for ten weeks; you are already too busy to take on anything else—look at your schedule; it's already full. This program will kill you; so it's not worth it!'

"I realized I was defeating the program for myself before I even started it. I was then instructed to get a thorough physical examination. I thought, 'That's my out; the doctor will see that my heart will not take that strenuous exercise, and that will let me out of it all.'

"Half hoping this would be the case, I went further and was examined carefully. But the doctor would not cooperate. My heart could take it. Realizing I had no valid excuses left, I began reminding myself I wanted to be physically fit and 'I am athletic!'—my new label.

"The first week was torturous, but my body responded quickly. In the ninth week I was able to bound up long flights of stairs two at a time and not only feel alive, but great, when I got to the top. I was able to run a mile each day during my lunch hour and to play racquet ball—and actually to win occasionally. Instead of dragging home from a long day at work, I was able to come home with renewed energy and enthusiasm. As of this writing, I have had enough energy to start up a private business after my regular working hours, and it has paid off. Imagine that! And I used to feel beat by five o'clock!" (Chamberlain, 1976.)

Another participant of this program, working on compulsive eating, lost twelve pounds in two weeks by looking at herself in the mirror several times a day and instead of saying the usual thing to herself, "You're a fat slob" (her negative label), she changed it to "You beautiful doll" (her new label). She reported that at first it sounded too unrealistic. But after trying it as an experiment for two weeks, she discovered that her "fat slob" self-image ate more than her "beautiful doll" self-image. She advised others, "Don't knock it until you've tried it."

That is my advice to you now: "Don't knock it until you have tried it." Experiment with it; let yourself think of yourself in a different way. This can be the beginnings of dropping your self-defeating behavior. It's really exciting when you feel changes actually taking place inside you over a period of time.

35

A Word About Negative Labels

The youngest of five boys in my own family and somewhat less athletically inclined than my older brothers, I was given to know in many ways that I was nonathletic. For example, even though I tried out for various teams, I was usually the first to be cut from the team by the coach. I was typically last to be chosen amid groans from the team that *had* to take me on their side. Even though I never gave up trying, I lived under the label: "I am nonathletic." I carried this label with me for about forty years, considering it to be a negative one. It became a self-fulfilling prophecy; that is, it remained so until I realized the power labels have in our lives and, more importantly, the relative ease with which they can be changed.

During all those years I used my label as a "cop-out" so that I would not have to try. I used it to keep me from learning how to play certain sports. When I was a young married man, whenever my friends asked me to come and play on a neighborhood team of some sort, I would always refer to my old negative label, telling myself: "You're nonathletic; you don't know how to do that; you would make too many mistakes, and they would laugh at you." Even though I wanted very much to participate, I would listen to these old fears and would choose to say: "No, I'm too busy doing ...." I allowed my old negative label to dictate my current behavior in each new moment of living. In reality, I had the physical and mental ability to learn almost any sport, but I shifted the responsibility for my current behavior in each instance to my old and useless label.

Changing what you tell yourself about yourself may seem so simple that you will not even want to try it to see what it can do for you, but if you remind yourself of your new label often enough, something will begin to change inside you, and you will feel it working for you.

I Disown Responsibility by Blaming Others and Circumstances

The second major way we disown responsibility is to shift the blame for our SDBs to someone or something outside ourselves. The following conversation indicates we came from a long line of "blamers," but disowning responsibility for our behavior in this way did not then, nor does it now, alter the consequences.

The Lord God: "Adam ... hast thou eaten of the tree, whereof I commanded thee that thou shouldest not eat?"

Adam: "The woman whom thou gavest to be with me, she gave me of the tree, and I did eat."

36

The Lord God:	(To the woman) "What is this that thou hast done?"
Eve:	"The serpent beguiled me, and I did eat." (Genesis 3:9-13.)

While these appear to be simple statements as to what happened, they also sound like excuse-making in which the finger of blame is pointed from one to the other and finally to "the serpent," or Satan. Yet in each "partaking," the two parents—Adam and Eve—had their agency to choose or not to choose to do it. You and I have the same agency, and we exercise it every day in what we choose to do. We would like to think we are not responsible for making these choices so that we can blame someone else for the results we get.

You must discover that you disown responsibility for your SDB by taking the responsibility for your behavior off yourself and placing it onto someone or something else. Some examples of what others have discovered may help you to see some of your own ways of disowning (Adapted from Cudney, note 1):

"It happens automatically. I'm not really in control."

"It's a habit I have. I habitually do it without thinking."

"I inherited my SDB, so it is a part of *me*."

Please take note that SDBs are *learned behaviors*. They are not inherited. We were born free of them and learned them in the process of maturing.

"I am different from other people—if they were like me, they would do it too." (Do I do my SDB to *maintain* this feeling of being different in this negative way?)

"I really don't do my SDB. It's my bad self or mood that does it, not *me*."

"My mother made me eat everything on my plate."

"My father expected me to be this way."

"My family is no good."

"That's how it's always been in the past."

"I take full responsibility for my SDB." (But I do it in such a way as to convince myself that as long as I *admit* I am responsible, that is all that is needed, and I can continue to do it.)

"He 'put me down' and gave me an inferiority complex."

"I can't control my feelings."

"That's just the way I am."

"I get relapses."

"I find myself depressed or nervous."

"My SDB has happened a few times."

"My problem is imbedded in me."

"The devil made me do it."

"I always work best under pressure."

"I was made this way."

Now make up a list of your disowning techniques. Use the lower part of the summary form you have made for Step Two. Become more aware of how you have used blaming and labeling in your life in the past, and attempt to catch yourself doing it in the present. Then take charge of the responsibility for doing your SDB. By doing this, you can begin to free yourself from it. You must own up to doing it and to the fact that it is *yours* before you can begin to get rid of it. You can't get rid of it if it belongs to someone else. That's *their* SDB, not yours. Also, assuming ownership for what you do will help those around you see more clearly their own responsibilities and can help them change their behaviors.

A final word about disowning responsibility. Disowning statements or thoughts come in many disguises. Whenever you think the behavior is not of your doing, or it just happens to you, or it is totally automatic, inherited, or beyond your control, these are disowning statements or thoughts.

When you disown responsibility for doing your SDB, you are really saying: "If others would change their behaviors, or if circumstances would be different, then I could change my behavior." Over the years, I have observed in my work with people that others do not change their behavior because I want them to. However, when I change *my* behavior, others react differently toward me, and in this way I can help bring about a change in those around me.

"For many years I struggled with the self-defeating behavior of my inability to say *no*. This behavior created havoc with my professional and private life. I felt I had no control over my own schedule because I would allow others (anyone who wanted my help) to usurp my time and energies because I feared saying no to additional requests. By so doing, I finally reached a point of trying to keep up with seven jobs in my church while working more than full time in the family dairy—all this while starting my married life.

" 'It's their fault. They shouldn't ask me,' I would tell my bride. 'If they would stop asking me to do so many things, I could stop doing them.' These were my disowning arguments. Years later, when I realized how I was keeping the problem going by these disowning statements, I began to see how I could shoulder the responsibility for my *own* behavior and to take charge of my *own* schedule. It is a great feeling to be in charge of my own life again!"(Chamberlain, 1976).

Nothing will be of any use to us unless we have taken the most important step of all: the decision to produce change inside ourselves. Not a change in my father or mother, not a change in my wife, husband, children, not in anyone else—in myself. Let us initiate change in ourselves, for then and then only shall we be able to effect a change in other people. (Huxley, 1971:7-8)

Some participants feel they have to wait until the end of the program to drop their SDB. You can stop doing your SDB any time you wish. If you are successful in dropping it so soon, so much the better. But continue with the remaining steps presented in the program to insure against relapses later on.

To complete this step, list on the summary form for Step Two as many ways as you can in which you disown responsibility for doing your SDB. Write in your diary for a few more days. Then follow instructions on how to critique what you have written before going on to Step Three.

STEP TWO SUMMARY FORM: HOW I DISOWN RESPONSIBILITY FOR DOING MY SDB   DATE_____

1. **My old and new label:**
   (a) _____
       My NEGATIVE LABEL, i.e., "I am a procrastinator."
   (b) _____
       My NEW LABEL, i.e., "I am well organized," or
       "I get things done on time," or "I *do* pro-
       crastination."

I will remind myself several times each day of my new label, and I will let myself think of me in this different way, even if at first it seems untrue and phoney.

2. **How I Shift the Blame:**
I will list below (or on a form similar to this that I have made) all the ways I disown responsibility for my self-defeating behavior. Who or what do I blame so that I can do it again?

_____
_____
_____
_____

_____
_____
_____
_____
_____
_____
_____
_____
_____
_____
_____
_____

(P.S. Don't forget your daily diary.)

Critique for Step Two

By the time you get to this point, you should have kept your daily diary for at least four to five days after completing your critique for Step One. You should also have observed yourself carefully to discover all the ways you have shifted or disowned responsibility for your SDB, including how you used to live under a negative label.

You will be given instructions in this section that will help you to go back over your own written statements in the same objective way you did in Step One. Some examples are shown to help you see what you can do with your list. Your purpose in doing this analysis is to help yourself "see through" some of your own behavior techniques that are aimed at helping you keep your SDB going.

Step Two Summary Form (Example SDB: *Compulsive Eating*)

Disowning Techniques I Use	*My Critique of My Disowning Techniques*
The smell of food in the house gets to me.	The smell of food *makes* me do my SDB? I *allow* it to do so.
My husband has to have foods not on my diet.	He or his needs make me do it? His food makes me do my SDB?
It's too hard to keep on my	My diet makes me do it? The

40

diet and cook for my family.

My children expect sweets and pastries.

hardness of it makes me do it?

My family makes me do it?

They make me do it? Their expectations make me do it? Or do I encourage them to *want* goodies so I can have them too?

(Example SDB: *Inferiority Feelings*)

Disowning Techniques I Use

My friend makes me feel inferior.

My Critique of My Disowning Techniques (Composite Entries)

He makes me do *my* SDB? I give him power over my behavior.)

My parents behave in inferior ways around people who have an education. I take after them.

My parents make me do it *now* in these fresh *new moments* of living? It's in my genes?

They taught me how to do it.

I *decide* to do my SDB because my parents did theirs?

I feel inferior in school-related situations.

School makes me do it? I *choose* to feel my SDB in these situations.

My boss makes me feel inferior when he talks to me or tells me to do something.

He makes me do it? (As long as I can blame him, I don't have to see what I do to keep my SDB or try to take control over my behavior.)

I blame the way I was raised.

My past makes me do it *now?*

I am no good at certain sports.

I *decide* to put others on a pedestal so I can feel inferior to them. It works! There is no

41

I tell myself they or he is better than I am.

way others can make me feel inferior unless *I decide to let them. I* am in charge of how I feel—*not they!*

People look at me as if I am dumb.

I decide what people think of me from my own feelings about myself, and then I react back to them as if *they* really thought those negative things about me! How sneaky!

Critiquing My Diary

In looking over your diary for Step Two, look for ways you have attempted to (a) shift the responsibility, and (b) rationalize away the adverse consequences of doing your SDB. Also look for points of time in your current life in which you apparently made a choice—a decision to do it again, or to do what would eventually lead into the doing of it again. Remember in your critique to insist that the writer of the diary assume more responsibility for what goes on.

DAILY DIARY (SDB: Procrastination)

January 10

My Critique

I determined yesterday that I was going to get up early this morning and get things done before the rush was on to get breakfast and to get the kids off to school and my husband to work by 8:00 a.m. But I was so upset at all the things I had to do that I tossed and turned all night until by morning I was exhausted. When the alarm went off, I just couldn't get up. So I slept in as usual, and my sweet husband got the kids ready for school and let me sleep until he left to go to work. Then I felt so depressed and bad that I couldn't make myself get out of bed and face the day. I also knew there would be a big mess in the kitchen with dirty dishes from yesterday, and the way my husband fixes breakfast is a

I decided to start "tomorrow." Tomorrow I will be a responsible person, but today I will avoid it. A good resolve, but. . . ?

I *made* myself upset by thinking about all I had to do and scaring myself with all that responsibility so that I would feel awful by morning. It worked! I could choose to take each task one at a time and be in charge of myself. I set myself up for this whole day then blamed the circumstances (which I created) so I could do my SDB.

I decided to feel so bad about what I didn't do that I

sight! I told myself it was just too hard for
me to keep up with all this; and I am so far
behind in everything—haven't washed
clothes for three weeks, and my mending
and cleaning are way behind.

I just lay there feeling so hopeless and
wishing I could get out of the whole mess
some way and still be respectable. I can't
imagine how my husband puts up with such
a dirty, messy house. His office is very
efficient and neat. He must hate me for
being so lazy. It seems I have not had any
motivation since I was sick two years ago. I
guess I sort of gave up then trying to keep
on top of things. I notice that I feel
defensive and angry whenever the children
make additional requests for my time and
energy. What do they all expect of me—to
be the bionic woman? My favorite soap
opera came on at 11:00 a.m. I argued with
myself that I deserved to get some
"enjoyment out of life." And besides,
watching TV might cheer me up. Then I'll
still have time to get the kitchen done
before 3:30 when the kids come home from
school. Later.

could use that feeling to decide to not do some more. In my mind, I made the mess in the kitchen seem too big to tackle so that I could have a "just cause" to not even start. I blamed *him* for making the mess that I should have made. I made it all hard and formidable for me so that I could do my SDB and feel justified.

I spend more time avoiding than doing the tasks at hand. I can *decide* to do one task at a time— that is all anybody can do!

I can choose to make this seeming mountain climb a downhill run by doing the biggest or hardest job first, then move on to the next easier one, and so on. In this way I can lighten my load earlier and live happier. I choose to compare myself to him in such a way that I can make myself feel down. I use that past event to serve *now* as a cop-out. I can feel that I don't even have to try; look how sick I was!

I know how to build up pressure by doing my SDB so that I can use anger to sidetrack the real issue at hand and keep my SDB going.

I tell myself that they all expect too much so that I can do even less than I am able to do. I decided to watch T.V. instead of doing the things I needed to do so that I could get myself feeling even worse.

The rest of the day was no different. I watched TV and felt worse and guilty besides. Then I ate a peanut butter sandwich and two glasses of cold chocolate milk—yuck! I started on my dishes when I remembered something else that needed to be done. I stopped and went from one thing to another until there was no time left to get the kitchen cleaned up. When my oldest daughter, Susie, came home from school, I told her to do the dishes for me because I was too busy on something else. She put up a fuss and cried, and I got upset with her for being so ungrateful that she can't even help out a little bit. We argued, and I finally ended up doing the dishes myself, with her sitting in her room mad and sulking. I hope I can overcome my problems. I know that I am causing others in the family to have problems. It's so hard for me to stick to this diary. I can think of at least 101 things I should be doing right now, and this isn't one of them. (Composite diary.)

I made certain the whole day was like this by the way I set it up. I *make* days turn out for me the way they do. I tell myself I don't even have time to eat decently.

I keep myself in a disorganized dither to keep my SDB going. It works great!

Now I try to shift more responsibility to others without letting them plan for it so that I can get them *and* me discouraged.

Can I ever expect "gratitude" from someone who is angry?

I should have decided long before now to dive in and get them done and saved myself a lot of worry and hard feelings between my daughter and me.

I want to change this unhappy state of affairs. I *am* changing it! I am trying to defeat this change program to keep my SDB intact. Not writing in my diary is one sure way of keeping the whole thing under cover with myself where I can't see what I am doing.

After critiquing your diary entries, feel free to go on to Step Three. Upon reaching this point in the program, many people experience the emergence of a new feeling. Some have expressed it as a new excitement for living, a feeling of success that leads them further—some of the fruits from the planting of a good seed. Others will not have tried to remind themselves of their new label because it seems too "simple." It is simple. But, not *too* simple. I suppose what they really mean is that "It is too ridiculous for a person of my stature to do something as simple as that." They are the ones who keep their SDBs going much longer. It does take some patience and diligence to reap the good results you want.

REFERENCES:

Chamberlain, Jonathan M.
1976 Eliminating a Self-Defeating Behavior. Handbook for Education 514Rx-1, a Brigham Young University Home Study Course: How to Eliminate a Self-Defeating Behavior. Fourth edition. Brigham Young University Printing Services, Provo, Utah.

Felker, Donald W.
1974 Building Positive Self-Concepts. Minneapolis, Minnesota: Burgess Publishing Company.

Huxley, Laura A.
1971 You Are Not the Target. North Hollywood, California: Wilshire Book Company.

STEP THREE:
WHAT PRICES
DO I PAY
FOR DOING MY
SELF-DEFEATING
BEHAVIOR?

YOUR OBJECTIVES FOR STEP THREE

You will be able to:
1. List the long- and short-range prices you pay for doing your self-defeating behavior, and the positive things you miss.
2. Recognize how much the SDB hurts you.
3. Discover and list the ways you minimize the prices you pay.
4. Use your own price list to determine if you can afford to do it.

HOW TO PROCEED

In order to achieve these objectives, you must complete the following activities:
1. Read "What Prices Do I Pay for Doing My SDB?" (following). Complete the assignments as they are given on the summary form for Step Three.
2. Continue to write in your daily diary.
3. After doing the reading, writing, and critiquing, you may go on to Step Four.

What Prices Do I Pay for Doing My SDB?

To fully appreciate the price concept developed in this step, you will have to understand on a deep level the penalty you pay for doing behaviors that interfere with your best self and its harmonious functioning. You were created to function successfully as part of an externally and internally congruent system. When you use self-defeating behaviors to cope with your world, you interfere with the harmonious operation of your creative human system.

Not only are you created to function best as a congruent person, but so is the culture in which you live and the world of which your culture is a part. Thus, when you use SDBs, you pay a very deep price, and, in ways that are not easily detected, so do your immediate family, friends, and the city, state, and country—in an ever-widening circle of influence. To clog up any part of the creative works of something is to interfere in some way with the whole system. When a cell in an organ of the body goes wrong, it affects adversely those cells surrounding it. They in turn affect those around them until the entire organ breaks down. Eventually the whole body may stop functioning.

As a rock that is dropped into a still pond of water in some predictable and systematic way moves all the molecules of water in the entire pond, so you as an individual create "waves" that directly or indirectly affect yourself first and all those around you, not only now, in the present, but also in the future. For example, the average alcoholic SDB of one person directly and adversely effects the lives of approximately 12 others. In many cases, this effect is the loss of self-respect or even a tragic death. In addition, indirectly all taxpayers and their families in the entire nation are affected by the expenses involved in treating, rehabilitating, salvaging, or rebuilding in the wake of that SDB. In 1975 the national bill in the United States for alcoholism was approximately 27 billion dollars. Yet, most individual drinkers firmly believe "It's nobody's business if I drink myself to death!"

Because of the nature of this harmonious life system in which we live, no person can be an island unto himself. As the molecules of water in a pond sustain each other, so do we as fellow human beings sustain and influence each other's lives in the physical and spiritual realms of our existence. We may never know in our lifetime the total effects we have had on the lives of countless others. We are also limited in foresight and knowledge regarding our own selves, partly because of the erroneous ideas we have learned about ourselves. We are as if living in our own small area of our pond, unable, at present, to take in the breathtaking views that lie just above and beyond the surface of our SDB-laden and limited existence. But now we are learning how to break through that over-protective barrier and emerge as our best selves.

There are natural laws that govern our life systems. When we become aware of them and put ourselves in tune with them, we can use them to our advantage and self-enhancement, for they were created for our positive use, to help us live successfully and happily.

The Law of "Blessings and Hurts"

There are laws man cannot change that govern what we receive in turn for our efforts and our behaviors, whether those behaviors are negative and self-defeating or positive and self-enhancing. As you proceed in this step of the program, I hope you will soon see clearly that you are very much in charge of what happens to you—that you are the one in charge of most of the positive results you receive as well as most of the "hurts" you get. The same natural law governs both your "blessings" and your "hurts." The determining factors in most cases that make the difference in whether you receive one or the other are your own behaviors and attitudes, and these are dictated by your choices. Now, we don't usually think of it in this way. We usually feel that we are powerless to get what we really want or need, that things just "happen" to us. We are not powerless! Indeed, because of the creative beings we truly are, we have great power, and it is at our disposal to use for our benefit and for those around us.

You will see that in most situations you are in charge of your own happiness as well as your own misery, that you hold the key as a free agent to go in either direction, and that you have power to act as well as to be acted upon.

Have you ever considered that human beings are the only creatures who have agency to choose? We can choose even to go against the laws of nature and our own well-being. All other creations go along with natural laws, whether by instinct or design, without the great variety of choice and the agency to choose. How we use our agency in moments of time is most crucial to our well-being. We can choose to work for or against the laws of good health, of financial success, of happy family life, and so on and on; but there will always be adverse consequences from negative choices because of these unchangeable laws. Like the laws that govern gravity, electricity, radio, and sound waves, they are here to stay, whether we recognize and accept them or not. When we understand these laws, we can then behave more intelligently and rationally for our own benefit.

The Law of Cause and Effect and of Recompense

Your behaviors, whether self-enhancing or self-defeating, have consequences that are inescapable. What you do makes a difference. You are unable to *not* make "waves." This is a universal law, a law of cause and effect.

Working together harmoniously and naturally with the law of cause and effect is another law that needs careful understanding. I call it the law of recompense. It simply means that what you give, you tend to get back, or "whatsoever a man soweth, that shall he also reap." (Gal. 6:7.) While you are totally in charge of the messages you send out, you cannot always control where or when the getting back or the reaping will occur; but get it back you will, sooner or later. Even a crime committed in secret, undetected by

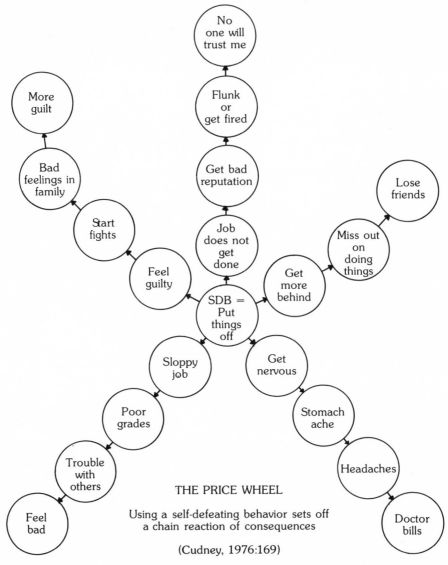

THE PRICE WHEEL

Using a self-defeating behavior sets off
a chain reaction of consequences

(Cudney, 1976:169)

50

our legal system, does not go unpaid for. There are inescapable natural consequences of all behavior, whether in the internal world of the person acting or in the external world acted upon. All actions set off chain reactions.

Human beings, as well as the microscopic atom and the larger kingdoms or systems with which man is acquainted, were created to work harmoniously together within these and other universal laws. When you exercise your agency to adhere to those laws, you receive happiness and fulfill the reason for your creation. But if you use self-defeating behaviors, you reap adverse consequences, which are the prices you pay for those behaviors. These consequences are self-defeating and hurting to us. It would be marvelous, some say, if we could eat all we want and not gain weight, or if we could do our sexual thing and not feel bad afterward. But that cannot be.

Just as there is no conceivable way that a rock dropped into a pond of water will not make an effect on most, if not all, of the

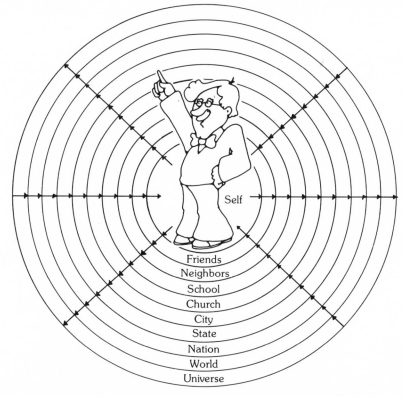

Your behavior makes a difference, and the effect is far-reaching.
You get back what you give.

51

molecules of water in the entire pond or system, so there is no way that your behavior will not have a consequence of some kind or another on yourself and on those around you, either now or later. You are in the important position to choose the effect it will have.

The consequences or prices suffered are inseparably linked to the action, or behavior. When you can clearly see this link between your behaviors and the prices you pay, you can more fully realize you are in charge of those prices; you are in charge of what happens to you.

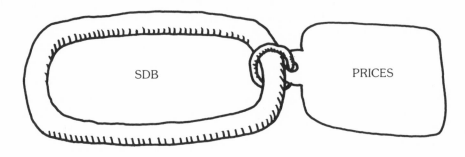

An SDB is inseparably linked with its prices

I experienced this principle of recompense in a positive way in my work with inmates at the Utah State Prison. I was able to feel genuine acceptance and respect for the inmates with whom I worked. In return, I was treated with the same acceptance and respect. Several commented on the noticeable difference in how I made them feel, compared to others who came there to "help" them. They expressed that they felt like human beings around me. These comments confirmed what I felt. I got back what I put out.

The Prices I Pay

Using SDBs is the same as maintaining a death system within yourself. SDBs kill energy and joy, consume time, destroy spontaneity, ruin relationships, contribute to poor health, cost money to maintain, and interfere with growth. Because of that inseparable link between the behavior and its consequences, it is not possible to use SDB patterns and not pay severe prices.

People who keep using self-defeating behaviors report some degree of unhappiness within themselves, an awful feeling of not being in full control of their lives, and a growing tiredness that increases as the behavior is continually used. Those who completely drop their self-defeating behaviors report a joy and a delight in being their best selves, with more meaning and peace in their lives. They tell of an ability to love more deeply, an eagerness for a new moment of living to come along, and a sense of freedom and control that comes from being at the helm of their own lives. We may not be able to recognize all the prices at this point. "When I used self-defeating behaviors, I paid some very deep prices; it was only after I let the behaviors go that life opened up for me, and I could truly see what the behaviors had cost me." (Cudney, note 1.)

Since becoming involved in this change program, you likely have some understanding of the cost for maintaining your SDB. However, you also likely have reasons for starting to use and continuing to use those behaviors. In order to let the SDB go, you need to deepen your understanding of the prices you pay as you use defeating behaviors. Exposing (for yourself to view) all the prices you pay is a good way to deepen this understanding and to internalize the consequences.

When you get to the point of letting the SDB go but can't seem to make the change, perhaps you have not fully owned up to this price concept. This concept, like the others, is easy to understand, but it must be internalized until you not only understand the prices but feel them as well—and feel them so deeply that there is no question about giving up the SDB. Let those prices work for you to convince you that the SDB *must* go.

The scale in the following illustration may be useful in helping you to understand this concept and the importance of the prices. As long as you use your SDB, you are saying you are better off *with* the behavior than *without* it. Facing the many prices you pay for doing it will help you tip the scale in the other direction. The prices, when fully listed, recognized, and deeply felt, can give you the energy and motivation to drop the SDB. On the other hand, the reasons you tell yourself as to *why* you do the SDB add weight to the wrong side of the scale and only help you keep it going.

You will soon be asked to write down the prices you pay for doing your SDB. After writing down and considering the prices carefully and openly, you will be asked to *feel* them. Then you will have all the more reasons for giving up the behavior that hurts you so much. At this point, an important concept to remember is that in almost all cases you can avoid paying any and all of those prices by dropping the SDB.

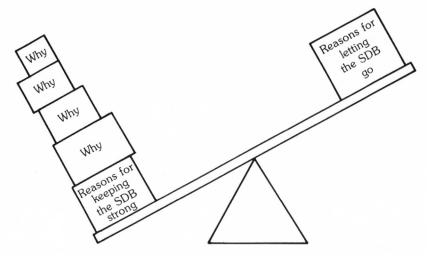

The scale has been tipped in the wrong direction.

Up to now you have apparently had more reasons for keeping your SDB than you have for giving it up. In other words, your reasons for keeping it going have outweighed the reasons you give yourself for letting it go. If this were not true, you would not be needing to work on this SDB at this moment. You would have already dropped the SDB from your pattern of behavior.

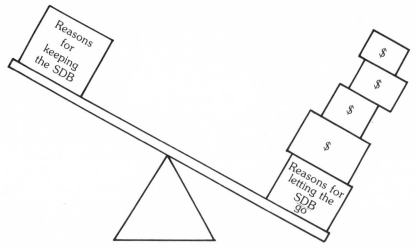

Tipping the scale in the right direction.

You can give yourself more reasons for letting go of the SDB by adding up your price list and stop rationalizing *why* you do it. Also, you can stop minimizing the prices you pay for doing it. When the full weight of those prices is felt, the scale will tip, and you will have more reasons for giving up the SDB than for keeping it.

How Do I Minimize My Prices?

After you identify the many prices (adverse consequences) you pay for doing your SDB and after you feel them at deeper levels than ever before, you will be asked to notice how you go about minimizing those prices when you are about to do your SDB again. It seems to be a normal behavior before doing an SDB to minimize the adverse consequences that will result from doing it, immediately afterward only to reap the full price that cannot be mitigated. After the act, you realize how you were fooling yourself by minimizing or rationalizing away the consequences in order to allow yourself to do it.

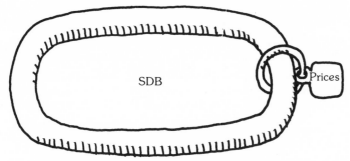

Anticipating the SDB *BEFORE* doing it, or MINIMIZING the prices

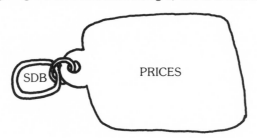

But *AFTER.* Was it really worth it?

When you minimize, you are partially blinding yourself. You allow yourself to see only what you want to see for the moment. It is possible, and wise, to view the SDB and its possible adverse consequences (the prices) *before* doing it and, in that second, also to weigh all those prices against doing the SDB. In this manner you can take advantage of the opportunity to choose more wisely the results you want for yourself. You are in charge of the results. You can choose the results you want.

You may discover additional prices later that you could not think of in your first effort to write them down. Continue to add to your list. Make it as long as you can. It must outweigh whatever reasons you have been using to continue the SDB. If you weigh the prices against doing the behavior and find that you *can* afford to do it, then keep adding to your price list until you realize that you *cannot* afford to do it any more. You are the only one who can convince yourself that the SDB must be eliminated.

There are several good reasons for listing all these consequences; and I hope your list will be at least twenty items in length. One reason is that normally, in the course of living with our SDBs, we may be aware of only two or three prices at any one time; we forget to remind ourselves of the many others attached to the SDB that hurt us a few days before or some time further in the past. Thus, by making a list and keeping it before you for several weeks, you can see the full array of consequences and recognize even more the cost to you of maintaining a behavior over which you are fully in charge. Another reason for listing consequences is that perhaps you have never before actually sat down and thought seriously of the results of the SDB you have been doing.

Positive Things Missed

This price list of consequences not only includes the adverse results in a short- and long-range view, but also the many positive things you miss out on because of it. For example, you may recognize that you are missing some important, desirable aspects of living, or that you are not obtaining worthwhile goals as long as you maintain the SDB. These "unreachables" could be yours if it were not for the SDB that keeps you from enjoying them. They too must be included in the cost to you for keeping the SDB going. Remember, you are the world's expert on the prices you pay for doing your particular SDB. They are *your* prices—no one else suffers from paying them as you do.

For many people, this step in the course is a turning point. Don't worry if your "adverse results" list and your list of "positive things missed" seem to get mixed up with each other; brainstorm and write down as many as you can think of. Later be alert to and add to your list any new ones you had missed.

Minimizing the Prices

Catching how you minimize the prices you pay may be a bit tricky. I believe that after you have completed your price list you cannot do a SDB again unless you in some way minimize that list of consequences in your own mind *before* you do it. It is a normal part of maintaining an SDB.

Several of the SDB participants at a state prison described the way they had minimized the price list for a criminal act. Minimizing allowed them to then go ahead and do the act with no serious thought about the possibility of any consequences other than the falsely positive ones they were hoping for. For this way of thinking, they were spending five to twenty-five years of their lives without personal freedom; they were suffering broken relationships with loved ones and loss of respect and trust. I have come to accept as a rule of thumb *that the more completely the individual minimizes away the consequences of the behavior, the more severe and adverse the consequences will be.*

Most of us do not have to be imprisoned formally to see clearly the prices we pay for our SDBs. There are other kinds of "prisons" we close upon ourselves, and they serve the same purposes—to inhibit, to stop or dam our progress, to restrict our inner and outer selves, and to keep us from reaching our potential even in the full light of free agency and choice. We may never know in this lifetime how far-reaching and costly some of these prices are! But we can get enough of a glimpse of them to let us know that already we have paid too much to want to continue in that behavioral direction.

Some participants at this point, after making out their price list, begin to tell themselves, "W-e-e-l-l, I don't need to work on my SDB any more. It's not *that* bad. I've lived with it for so long now ...." These are signs that they would like to defeat the change program and keep the SDB. Usually this occurs when the person can see somewhat more clearly than ever before that the behavior has got to go; but, if it does, then what? The uncertainty represented in that question is a bit unsettling to some.

If this occurs to you, don't let it stop you now. This program is designed to cope with uncertainty. Keep taking the next step that leads to victory. The battle may be half won by now. It is normal to experience some apprehension and even anxiety about giving up the behavior at this point. In some ways it is beneficial to feel apprehensive in order to make the change you really want to make. If you feel these things, you are right on target; but if you don't feel them, don't be concerned.

When you fully realize that you get back what you give (the law of recompense), you can understand that you, not others, are in charge of your own destiny and the consequences of your behavior.

57

A very beautiful, dark-haired young girl in her late teens dressed up to go to the local dance. However, she believed she was not beautiful and that boys would not like her. So at the dance she would sit on the sidelines, and the girls on either side of her would get asked to dance, but she would not.

She carried her negative fears and feelings about herself on her face. Boys, without any prior training in human behavior, would read that nonverbal message and steer clear of her. And to some, the message came across, "Stay away from me, you creep!" Real anger and hostility finally welled up inside this girl to the point that after putting up with this "rejection" from those "dumb boys" as long as she could, she stomped out of the dance hall and walked home, vowing never to go back again.

When she realized that *she* was in charge of the boys' reactions to her, things began to change. Like many newcomers on the social scene, she had been fearful that boys would notice her, then fearful that they would not. She allowed these fears to dictate her behavior toward them and to create unpleasant and strained feelings. She also used the technique of doing their thinking for them by telling herself they would not like her and then behaving toward them as if these negative self-thoughts were really theirs—not hers.

Be aware of how the "law of recompense" and the law of "cause and effect" work in your own life so that you either get hurtful results or self-enhancing results. But most important of all, realize that you are the person in charge of what you get back. If your life is miserable, take note of what you do to make it that way. If it is happy, be aware of what you do to make it that way. Love engenders love, and kindness engenders kindness.

To complete this step and to apply the concepts presented here, fill in the following activities on the two Step Three summary forms. Do each one before proceeding to the next.

First, on Summary form A for Step Three list all the short-range and far-reaching prices you pay for doing your SDB. Dig deeper than ever before so that you will be thorough in this effort to include adverse results. Include all the positive or good things you would like to have or do, but that you miss out on because of your SDB. *(Put a copy of this list of prices where you will see it often.)*

Second, take a few quiet moments to meditate on those prices; let yourself feel and know how much they hurt you.

Third, on Summary form B list ways you have attempted to minimize these prices. You can discover these from the question: "What things do I tell myself that make paying the prices seem so unlikely, or remote, or not at all, so much that I can justify doing the SDB again?" Knowing the prices you pay, there is no way you can continue to do your SDB unless you minimize these prices. Being fully aware of how you minimize is important in giving up this behavior. Once you recognize what these ways are, try to take control over your minimizing thoughts or statements. Don't be surprised if you find that some are irrational ways of thinking.

Examples of Prices Paid and Positive Things Given Up

Following are some examples of how others have done the above activities:

Prices I Pay for Using My SDB

- I am unable to be fully happy with myself
- Depression
- Impaired relationships
- Living with fear
- Poor health and expected early death
- Unnecessary expenditure of money
- A giving-up kind of tiredness from carrying around a SDB
- Contributing to hurt in others and getting in the way of their growth
- Dearth of energy, time, and spontaneity
- Shame for myself as I use the behavior
- Negative contributions (if only in very tiny ways) to all the systems I am part of: family, church, school, city.
- Loss of full control over my life
- Inability to fully know myself as a person

Positive Things I Miss Because of My SDB

- Increased time and energy to do important things
- An ability to accept myself as a person and be happy with myself
- More meaning and peace within
- A deeper ability to love
- Eagerness for a new day to dawn and looking forward to new, unknown moments of living
- An ability to live in the now, fully, without holding back
- A sense of freedom by being at the helm of my own life
- Increased production at work, home, and play
- Openness to growth

- An ability to experience in a life-giving manner the full range of emotions from joy to grief
- A positive impact on the lives of others
- A life of progression

Keep your personal list before you as a constant reminder. Add to your list as you become aware of new prices.

Examples of How I Minimize the Prices I Pay for Doing My SDB So That I May Continue It

- I keep busy and occupied as a way to avoid facing those prices.
- I joke about the prices to try to make them seem less severe.
- I compare my prices with the prices of others in such a way that mine don't appear so severe after all and especially not so severe as theirs.
- I perceive prices to be beneficial; for instance, I create tension, then convince myself I can't function without it.
- I turn my head to the pain I inflict on other people.
- I perceive prices as something that can't be avoided; that's the way of life.
- I function at 50 percent capacity or less and tell myself this is all my life energy will permit at the present.
- I get engrossed in the problems and hangups of other people in order to turn away from facing the prices I pay within myself.
- I consider real freedom from this SDB as an impossibility, and then I don't look at what I do to restrict freedom in myself.
- I say to myself that these problems will someday go away, or I probably won't have them in the grave.
- I tell myself I need those prices to convince myself I must be a tremendous person or I couldn't put up with so much.
- I constantly make apologies for my behavior (or its results) and the prices; then I think that takes me off the hook for the hurtful things I do to myself and others.
- I conclude that it was predestined to be that way. That's the way it is; that's the way God made it. In this way I rationalize the prices I create.
- I build a way of life around them and adapt to them so that I don't have to give them up.
- I ignore that I am being hurt.—(Adapted from Cudney, note 1.)

If you want to rid yourself of ill-fitting repeatable behavior patterns, you must let the prices you pay and the prices others pay because of your SDB do their job. When you have done these four activities, no way remains for you to ward off or minimize the prices, and they will bring you to a deep realization of their effects in your life. When that happens, the motivation and courage will be present in you to face the fears and get rid of the SDB.

It is important to keep your price list in front of you for several weeks as a constant reminder. "Those are the prices I pay for doing my SDB. They are not worth it!" You may find it helpful to put colored paper squares or the actual price list on the mirror or on the refrigerator door, in a notebook, a wallet, or a purse as a reminder of what you only are paying. No one else pays your prices.

Whenever you are tempted to relapse or to waver and do your SDB again, first and quickly get out your price list and see if you can afford it. If you discover you can, look at how you are minimizing those prices in order to distort reality so that you can rationalize yourself into doing it again. You can stop the minimizing process by recognizing how you do it and deciding to look ahead at the true prices that must be paid. You know what they are now from past experiences. You can no longer continue to fool yourself.

When you have completed this lesson, there should be little question in your mind that you must give up your self-defeating behavior. If there is still some doubt, add more to your price list until you are convinced the SDB has *got to go!*

That SDB Has *GOT* to Go!

If, after making the list of prices, feeling them on deeper levels, and convincing yourself that you must tip the scales once and for all, you still use the SDB, don't allow yourself to feel discouraged; there are yet some other important factors to consider in the steps to follow. We are zeroing in on the enemy.

STEP THREE SUMMARY FORM A: THE PRICES I PAY FOR DOING MY SDB   DATE_____

List (either on this form or a similar one you have devised) the prices you pay for continuing your self-defeating behavior. Include (a) the short- and long-range adverse results, and (b) the positive things you are missing by doing your SDB.

A._____
_____
_____
_____
_____
_____
_____
_____
_____
_____
_____
_____

B._____
_____
_____
_____
_____
_____
_____
_____
_____
_____
_____
_____
_____
_____
_____

STEP THREE SUMMARY FORM B: HOW I MINIMIZE THE PRICES I PAY   DATE_____

List below the ways you have minimized your prices in the past or have attempted to do so during this program. (How do you try to rationalize away the prices?)

_____
_____
_____
_____
_____
_____
_____
_____
_____
_____
_____
_____
_____
_____
_____
_____
_____
_____
_____
_____
_____
_____
_____
_____
_____
_____
_____
_____

Critique For Step Three

Before going on to Step Four, take a look at what you have written for Step Three. There is not much else to do with your price list (Summary Forms A and B), but you can keep it handy and add to the list any new ones you may discover later on. The price list does not necessarily change your SDB, but it certainly can go a long way toward providing the needed incentive to want to give it up. When you are thoroughly convinced that the prices you pay are not worth keeping the SDB, you are ready to make some changes; but don't wait until then to continue this program. Keep going.

DAILY DIARY (SDB: sexual self-abuse) January 30

My Critique

I am beginning to feel a little depressed at all the prices I have been paying. I never realized how sneaky I have been trying to hide all that from myself to keep doing my SDB and kidding myself that it didn't really hurt me to do it. It has been an eye-opener to come to face this in myself and a somewhat humbling experience. Since Step Two, I can't even blame anything else for it. I really am my own worst enemy. I decided that I deserve better treatment than I have been giving myself.

I *made* myself feel depressed by looking carefully at the consequences of SDB.

I am learning more about myself and how I have set myself up for a way of thinking that helps me to rationalize and keep my SDB going.

I am learning that *I* am really responsible for all I do. Taking that responsibility is a way to free myself, but a little scary.

Today I kept my price list handy, and I even caught myself starting to minimize and rationalize those dumb prices away. And I was so sneaky about the way I did it. I told myself that since that was a list that I made myself, it wasn't anything really new, and besides, I was in control of the whole thing anyway so I could go ahead and do my SDB. When I was getting myself ready to do it, I realized that by that time I had almost blocked out of my mind all the consequences in my anticipation for another sexual experience. I had actually thrown the whole price list out of my mind as if it didn't even exist in order to go ahead with a "clear conscience" with my SDB.

Great! I am learning what it takes to apply these principles.

Excellent! I caught myself right in the act!

Minimizing could be done so quickly that I had to really be on my toes to catch me doing it.

I know now how important it is to catch myself rationalizing away the consequences *before* I do the SDB.

64

When I suddenly caught myself just in
time with the realization that I was kidding
myself again and that those prices won't go
away just because I minimize them out of
my mind, I had a flash of insight as to how
badly I would feel after I had finished. The
whole price list seemed to hit me right in
the stomach. I suddenly lost all my desire to
do it, and got myself under control just in
time to stop. I then decided to do my
studies and keep my mind on them. I felt I
had really won a major victory over my
SDB! That was the first time in my long-
standing habit that I had been able to stop
myself and take control. I will keep my price
list where I can see it frequently—especially
in the bathroom. (Composite diary.)

Sure I wanted to go ahead and do it anyway because it feels good, but I allowed myself to look down the road a few moments ahead and see what I was heading for. I'd been there before, and I knew it wasn't where I wanted to be.

Congratulations! Now watch out for a sneaky relapse.

Being in charge has its own reward.

STEP THREE SUMMARY FORM A

Example: (SDB: sexual self-abuse)

The Prices I Pay for Doing My SDB:

A: (Composite male entries): Guilt feelings, lack of self-respect, prevention from being motivated to succeed, time lost doing my SDB, loss of energy, feelings of inferiority, increased anxiety, interference with my growth as a person and with my relationship with others, loss of control over my life, depression.

A: (Composite female entries): Insecurity, negative self-attitude, negative thoughts, negative talk, inability to relate to others, anxiety, nervousness, lack of trust in others, self-criticism, poor self-image, lack of faith in self, fear of failing, self-pity, feeling "not good enough," discouragement, fear of what others will think of me, self-disgust, desire to run away, suicidal thoughts.

Positive Things I Miss Because of My SDB:

B: (Composite male entries): Spiritual growth, being outgoing, feelings of self-control, better relationships with opposite sex, time for more constructive thoughts and acts, more energy to try harder at work, seeing others as normal people rather than as sex objects, greater emotional involvement with others, increased productivity on the job, ability to accept myself and to grow, a sense of freedom, an ability to help others and society.

B: (Composite female entries): A better self-image, improved spiritual growth, clear conscience, more time for useful projects, honesty with myself, having more time for beautiful hands and fingernails, looking and feeling beautiful rather than ugly, pride in myself as a person and especially as a woman, mind and body control.

STEP THREE SUMMARY FORM B

How I Minimize the Prices I Pay

Example: (SDB: sexual self-abuse)

(Composite male entries): I tell myself I can take the time to do it. I tell myself I can quit any time if I really want to. I let the thoughts of the pleasure of it block out the consequences. I tell myself I have earned this as a reward when I abstain for a while. I tell myself there is nothing better to do. I think there is something wrong with me, or I could stop. It's a "natural" thing to do.

(Composite female entries): I am too "bad" to change. I will fail at anything I try, even getting rid of this SDB. This habit is too deeply ingrained in my way of life. I'll do it once more to see if I really can, or if it will feel the same. I don't trust feeling happy without my SDB. Why make a big deal out of it? It makes me feel less responsible and helps me forget my problems. I am not strong enough to resist the urge.

DAILY DIARY (SDB: temper tantrums; excessive anger) February 1

My Critique

I have been saying my new label several times a day, and it has helped me already. I have been telling myself "How patient I am" whenever little things come up that used to set me on a rampage. This morning I was wearing the new shoes I got for Christmas and was on my way to work in my best suit. When I stepped out the door, the dog (Labrador) jumped on me. He had been wallowing in the mud from an early thaw. Before I could stop him, he landed on my

Great going! I am applying what I have learned. Being positive makes me feel better about myself.

66

new shoes and plastered them with sticky mud. I started to raise my hand to slug him on the head and call him some names. When I thought of my new label and yelled at him "How patient I am!" it was so ridiculous that I burst out laughing and simply grabbed him by the collar and locked him up in his pen. I was still so shocked at my atypical reaction that when I saw someone had left his gate open, I didn't swear at the kids or the gate, but said again, "How patient I am." Then I did what I had to do—cleaned my shoes off and went to work. It can't be that simple to change a behavior like mine! I have never in my life laughed at mud on my new shoes before. The more I thought about it, the more I laughed on my way to work. My whole day was great! No one at work got on my nerves, and I kept my cool even when a fellow worker tried to get me angry by telling me about a mistake that was my fault. I told myself my new label and almost laughed in his face. I was able to see clearly what had happened and pointed it out to him; we parted with friendly feelings instead of anger and accusations as in the past. I realize that my SDB has kept me from solving problems effectively by attacking defensively the people involved instead of looking more objectively for the solution to the problem. It makes me indignant with myself to realize that I have been a problem for people for too long. I felt like old Scrooge when he finally saw the light. But now I'm wondering if it will really last. What about tomorrow? I can't have changed this easily. Have I been tricked?

I decided to use my new label and was surprised to find the effect it had on my feelings about a very serious situation.

I need to make it harder for myself!

I couldn't feature the change those simple words made in my behavior.

I decided to be my best regardless of *his* behavior! I am in control of me! No one can make me angry unless I choose to let them!

I am making progress!

Great insight!

I feel ashamed to recognize what suffering my behavior must have caused others around me.

I don't trust the simplicity of this. It must be more complicated and hidden than this. Am I trying to make it more difficult than it really is?

February 2

It was a bad day again. Before 8:00 a.m. I yelled at my wife, kicked my boy across the room, and threw a book at my daughter (fortunately I missed). I have spent the rest of the day feeling deeply remorseful, and I wonder if I can ever change. I felt I had to do something to make it up to my family, and so I called them from work and apologized. Later I took them all out for dinner.

I do this pattern of action, then catch myself after it is too late. I *can* choose to catch myself *before* I do it, and keep my prices handy before I do it. It only takes a second to think of the coming feelings of remorse.

What an expensive SDB! What a quiet dinner! Everyone was on guard. I keep telling myself this makes it all right again, but I know deep down inside it doesn't. My children are afraid of me—their own father! I'm sure they are wondering when I'm going to explode next. Tonight I realized I had not said my new label once today. I'm going to say it while I go to sleep and all day tomorrow and live up to it! I must: *the prices are too high!* (Composite diary.)

I am realizing even more that I've got to change this SDB! I don't want to be this kind of man! I am learning what it takes to change. Hang in there!

Do I use this uncertainty and my strength of force to get my way? Is this the only way I get my wants, by acting irresponsibly? I am learning how much control I really do have. I set myself up for this day's bad events. By not planning to take charge over my SDB I literally allowed myself to do it. Am I a child abuser? I read that over 10,000 children a year are killed by their own parents in moments of rage. I *must* control myself.

Reference Notes:

1. Cudney, Milton R.

    1971 Elimination of Self-defeating Behavior. Unpublished paper, Western Michigan University, Kalamazoo, Michigan.

References:

Chamberlain, Jonathan M.

1976 Eliminating a Self-Defeating Behavior. Handbook for Education 514Rx-1, a Brigham Young University Home Study Course: How to Eliminate a Self-Defeating Behavior, Fourth edition. Brigham Young University Printing Services, Provo, Utah.

Cudney, Milton R.

1976 Implementation and Innovation. Kalamazoo, Michigan: Life Giving Enterprises.

STEP FOUR:
WHAT CHOICES
DO I MAKE
TO ACTIVATE
MY SELF-DEFEATING
BEHAVIOR?

You have just completed one of the most difficult steps in the whole program—that is, if you have done Step Three as directed. Step Four will be eye-opening, even rewarding.

YOUR OBJECTIVES FOR STEP FOUR

You will be able to:

1. Recognize and state the *inner choices* you make to activate your self-defeating behavior and the choices necessary for dropping it.
2. Identify and state the *outer choices* you make to help your self-defeating behavior "happen" again.
3. Pre-experience yourself taking control over your self-defeating behavior in real life situations.
4. Recognize where you are at any given moment on your road map of life.

HOW TO PROCEED

To achieve these objectives, do the following:

1. Read "What Choices Do I Make to Activate My SDB?" and "About Those Choices," (following) and complete the assignments as they are given.
2. Continue your daily diary.

When you have applied Step Four for three to four days and have critiqued your diary, go on to Step Five.

What Choices Do I Make to Activate My SDB?

A self-defeating behavior does not happen on its own. Each time you use a SDB, several choices are required to activate it, and repetitive choices are needed to keep it going.

It is important to distinguish between two areas of choice: (1) the inner and (2) the outer choices. The inner choice is usually made before you are confronted with a situation that demands a response. You can ask yourself, "Will I decide to respond in that situation as just me, without any defeating behaviors; or will I undermine myself by not responding as my best and most complete self?" This inner choice is connected to daring to be completely your best in a moment of living. For instance: "Do I dare test out my abilities?" "Do I dare see just how adequate I am as a male or female?" "Do I dare put my ability as a writer, painter, student, parent, or worker on the line?" "Do I dare test out my strengths?"

Once you have made the inner choice, the stage is set for outer choices, which are needed to carry out the inner decision. If the inner decision is that you won't test your intelligence, you will have to make decisions to put tasks off, not to finish assignments, and to do only a partial job in situations that test your mental ability. If your inner decision is that you will not trust your own judgment on something, outer choices are required to manipulate other people to decide for you. If an inner choice is to not be as attractive a person as you can be, outer choices are made to take on excessive weight, maintain hostility, and misinterpret how other people respond. (Cudney, note 1.) If your inner choice is to remain single, outer choices are required to prevent marriage by your always "playing the field to find the right one"; seeing eligible candidates as threatening or too good, too old, too young; or seeing yourself as inadequate.

You can usually determine what your inner choice was by its outer manifestations—the results—each time the behavioral cycle is repeated. You do not arrive where you do by chance. You get there by a series of choices. This step in the program is designed to help you become aware of the choices you make to keep your SDB going and to open up to your view some alternative choices that could be made to keep you from doing the SDB. If you continually defeat yourself in areas that require you to use your intelligence, your inner choice may be to avoid seeing how intelligent you are. By alienating members of the opposite sex before the relationship can deepen, you are likely choosing to avoid testing your adequacy to get along with another person. Using behaviors to withdraw and avoid other people keeps you from seeing how acceptable you are to them. By being dependent on the ideas of others, you choose not to find out how good or bad your own ideas are.

Trying to change a SDB in the outer choice area is not the best way to go about it. Making changes in the outer choice area is possible, but more difficult. You make inner choices to respond in a SDB way *prior* to a given situation. By making the inner choice to do it again, you put yourself on a mental route, the other end of which is doing the SDB and paying all those prices waiting there to be paid. Once this route is taken and momentum is gained, trying to change directions at the outer choice level becomes much more difficult. The closer you come (to the goal), the harder it is to stop, until finally a point of no return has been reached and you have done it again.

My Road Map of Life

You must become aware that you make a decision *not* to confront a given situation as your best and integrated self, but to use a SDB instead that keeps you from your integrated self. At the moment the choice is made, realize you have power over the choice. A sense of helplessness comes from making SDB choices and not realizing you are doing this. On the other hand, a sense of control over your own life comes from the knowledge that you have power over choosing to go either on the SDB or on the creative, non-SDB route. When you see clearly that you can choose either route, you stand at the moment of behavior change and freedom from your SDB (see illustration of My Road Map of Life).

You can make inner and outer choices only in moments of time. Either kind of choice can be controlled easily in that moment in which it first occurs. You are going down the freeway of life ticking off mileage at a rapid but measured rate (60 seconds every minute). From your past experience, you know the situations coming up that demand a decision. You have already decided how you will behave in the face of these situations. When you do a SDB, it is because you choose to do it in one or more of these moments, or it would never be done. But even after making an inner choice to do it again, you can catch yourself in that next moment and change directions to the non-SDB route.

Traveling the SDB route occurs in cycles of varying lengths—for some SDBs, such as a temper tantrum, it may be over in a matter of a few seconds; with other SDBs it may take over a month.

73

My Road Map of Life

74

While this ability to change routes is within all of us, certain SDBs make it most difficult, if not impossible, to change once the first step in the SDB direction has been taken. For example, the person suffering with the SDB of severe alcoholism usually loses his freedom to choose not to drink once he has taken the first drink. This is partly due to the deadening effect the first drink of alcohol has on the brain cells, making the person less able to function in a normal way and deadening the reasoning and inhibitory centers in the brain. Thus we often hear a person who is totally inebriated say, "I only had one drink." He may be *aware* of only one drink—the first one. A somewhat similar condition that temporarily takes away the individual's agency to choose is found in the effects on the brain of certain mind-altering drugs, as well as those that are physically addicting. Because of these effects, the only sure choice that people with these SDBs have open to them is the inner choice to take or not to take the *first* one. The person's ability to make a correction from the SDB to the non-SDB route or to decide "how much" or "whether or not" is significantly watered down after the physical effects of the first one are in operation on the brain.

Because you are a free agent (you have freedom of behavioral choice in any moment of time), you can exercise that agency and take control over the choices open to you in any moment of living.

At first it may be difficult to take this control beforehand because it may be difficult to recognize at which point in time you made the inner choice to do your SDB again. If it is too difficult to catch before it happens, you can often find this crucial moment by backtracking to discover how you put yourself onto the SDB route again. You can then recognize the "road signs" that led you into it and supported the inner choice. As you backtrack carefully, you can also discover alternate routes (or ways of behaving) that are nonself-defeating. The more self-enhancing alternatives open to you, the easier it will be to choose one of them and to be your best self in that situation.

Recognizing and Controlling My Choices

Why is it sometimes difficult to control choices? Apparently, assuming full responsibility for personal choice is frightening to some people because they have many ways of disowning their choices, or even disowning that they do indeed choose. Also, in our culture we are often taught that it is best not to trust our own judgment. Too often we are led to believe that trusting only in sources outside ourselves is better than trusting ourselves.

75

Another reason we fail to recognize our inner choice is that in our culture we are taught to focus on and live in the outer area of doing, performing, and acting, rather than spending time probing the inner world of thinking and feeling. We can take the time to meditate to find our deeply-felt values and priorities. When we don't, we make a number of inner choices, and because we are largely unfamiliar with our world within, not even recognize that we are choosing. If a person always focuses on happenings outside his own mind, he will not be in touch with what happens within it. Getting in touch with yourself is more rewarding. (Adapted from Cudney, note 1.)

"Each man has a continent of undiscovered character within himself. Happy is he that acts the Columbus to his own soul." (Anonymous.) Also, that choices are made in a fraction of a second can make difficult catching yourself actually choosing. Thus, a choice can be made so fast that you can believe it just "happened," that it was not under your control.

Finally, if you have done an SDB for a good many years, you may come to believe that the behavior is just part of you and not something you *do*. By maintaining this erroneous perception, you do not recognize the choices *you* make that activate and keep the SDB alive. But remember that your SDB is not part of you, nor can it be—you were created without it.

You make five major choices in order to keep your SDB going. All of them are within your control:

1. You must make the inner choice to activate your SDB.
2. You must choose to carry out the inner choice in a series of outer movements or feelings (the outer choices).
3. You must choose to minimize the prices that will be paid for doing it again.
4. You must choose to abandon your best, most integrated self to go along the SDB route. Every time you choose to be on the SDB route, you are giving up something that is best and good in you to do it, and you hurt your best self to some degree by doing so.
5. You must in some way choose to disown responsibility for your own behavior and at least temporarily behave irresponsibly to get it done. In full knowledge of the fact that you are the doer of your SDB and of the consequent prices you will pay for it, it could be considered irresponsible of you to do it again.

When you take control over any or all of these choices, you are in control of your SDB. Remember, you were created to go straight

76

ahead on the non-SDB road, which leads to more happiness and freedom.

To gain full power over eliminating a SDB, you need to control fully your choices by completing the following activities:

First: Recognize that you make inner and outer choices to do your SDB by writing on the summary form for Step Four the inner and outer choices you have been making to do and to maintain your SDB. Also list some possible alternatives. You must not only see yourself as a chooser; you must also see that you make choices to put your self-defeating behavior patterns into gear.

Second: In a moment of living, catch yourself making the SDB choice and be aware of its alternatives. In this way you can become familiar with how you use your SDB patterns in specific situations in your life.

Third: When you come to a new moment of living or a situation in which you previously would have used your SDB, practice making non-SDB choices. Do this any time you can, and don't be discouraged if immediate progress is not obtained. Stop a moment and meditate; be fully aware of the choice-options you have open to you—which are on either the SDB route or the non-SDB route.

Fourth: Anticipate situations in which you have used SDBs before. Monitor yourself in these situations and watch for your defeating choices. Catch yourself making these choices, then consciously and purposefully make alternative self-enhancing ones instead.

Fifth: Try to lessen the time between your making a choice and your recognition of having made that choice. Get ahead of your own game.

Sixth: If you suffer a relapse, be very much aware of what you have done and learn from the relapse as much as you can. It is like learning to pay attention to the road warning signs that lead you onto the SDB route: quit making the choices that put fear into operation in these new moments of living. Realize that any fear you feel will direct your behavior in the SDB direction, rather than letting you direct and take control over your best self-behavior. Fear is only a technique you use to keep your SDB going.

Seventh: Pre-experience. Take a few minutes before each day begins or before a recurring SDB situation arises. Close your eyes and visualize or imagine yourself in that situation. See yourself responding as your best, non-SDB, or more integrated self, going down the non-SDB route in control of yourself.

Seeing yourself *before the event* and responding in this way can be of tremendous help when (and if) you find yourself in the actual situation. By doing this, you will have already experienced some of the feelings of being there as your best self, and the new route won't seem so strange when you get there. By doing this, you are "psyching yourself up" in a positive way so that you can do your best and be your integrated self in that moment of living. Many winning athletes and performers do this just before a contest. Seeing yourself "winning" in this struggle to change ahead of the real situations can be of tremendous help to you.

You already have the ability to pre-experience, or you could not end up doing your SDB because it takes imagining and planning to maintain any SDB.

Pre-Experiencing

I have found over a period of many years that it is extremely beneficial to meditate and pre-experience privately about the events of the oncoming day. In order to do this, I have made it a practice to arise earlier than my family so that I can allow time enough to know that I have come into touch with my best self and perhaps a divine source outside myself. For some, the best time may be later in the day or in the evening before going to bed. This private time can be used in pre-experiencing the events of the coming day in the imagination. You can do this because events of most days are quite predictable. The same kinds of things usually take place. You live a fairly well established daily routine, and you know from past experience on your road of life where the dangerous or tempting situations will be before you arrive at those points. Thus a few moments of preplanning in a pre-experiencing session can be *most* beneficial. This method provides a self-accounting and a time for evaluation, meditation, and reflection to recount verbally and mentally your efforts of the preceding day, including successes and relapses. It provides an opportunity to examine closely what went right or how you did a relapse, if you did. It opens up the opportunity to learn much more from your own life experiences and to gain needed insight into your own behavior. Like the instant replay on television, this reflecting time is helpful to see what happened and to learn what could be done to improve upon your performance.

Care must be exercised while pre-experiencing to not allow yourself to pre-experience the negative scene in which you do your SDB but to make certain you see yourself on the non-SDB route being your best self in a tempting situation or avoiding temptations altogether by paying no attention to them.

Unfortunately, many people think that pre-experiencing is too simple to be of any use in overcoming a SDB. But it seems there is more power in the simple things than we realize. Remember that the greatest power discovered by man is also the smallest thing discovered by man—the atom. With this discovery came another—that he who understands and controls the smallest unit has the most power. As it takes thoughtful care and planning to create something of value, so does it take thought and planning to make a period of time called a day a happy one.

Days are only days (periods of time). What you make of them is up to you. Instead of saying "it was a bad day," you can begin to assume more responsibility for your own behavior by saying "I made it a bad day." Then you can choose to have the kind of day that you want to have by choosing to be in charge of yourself in the small moments of time, in which you have perfect agency, to make up the day. When you are in charge of these moments, you are in charge of the day.

Pre-experiencing and committing your inner choices and your whole self along the non-SDB route can help you take control over your behavior in moments of time. In these quiet moments you can make some of the most important choices of your life.

About Those Choices

To illustrate how important the inner choices are and how seemingly automatically they are made, imagine with me for a moment that you have a desire or a need to go somewhere in your car—some place you have been many times before—perhaps to work. The inner choice to go there is made in a split second of time. It is made in your mind or in your thoughts. But deciding to go to your destination does not, by itself, get you there. You must somehow get out of the house and into your car—open the doors and do many other outer movements in order to get yourself to your destination. Along the way, you likely come to intersections and forks in the road where you must turn either one way or the other. You cannot go both directions, and you cannot go neither; you must go one of those ways, and you have already decided (usually before getting into your car) which road you will take at the fork or intersection. You take the one that leads most logically to your destination. If you have traveled this route many times, you likely do it without much thought, and you soon arrive at your destination.

The same is true of our inner and outer choices to do our SDBs. Examples: "I caught myself, after leaving the classroom, thinking that I would have a week to do my assignment, and I caught myself deciding right then to procrastinate until next week in getting my assignment done, when I knew all along that that is my SDB. I determined at that moment to go home and get it done, then relax all week instead of paying those horrible torturesome prices all week, then doing a half-baked job of it the night before and having to offer some flimsy excuse for doing less than my best."

"I did my SDB again. And it was not until I had done it that I realized how far and how quickly I had gone down my SDB road. I began to backtrack and try to figure out when I had made my inner choice to do it again. I discovered a very interesting thing. It was when I allowed myself to feel disappointed at what my 'friend' said to me. That was when I decided to do it again, and from that moment on I set myself up with a series of outer choices to see that I got it done. Although I did a relapse, I learned so much from this experience now that I have a 'road-map' to look at."

"Catching that moment of inner choice and taking charge over it gave me such a feeling of freedom as I have never experienced before. It made the whole thing seem so simple. I had been trying to make it too complicated and hard."

"When I could look ahead and see the fork in the road (the situation) coming, I could see more clearly which way I really needed to go to not do my SDB again; I didn't catch when I made my inner choice to do it, but I did switch tracks in my outer choice area and went down the non-SDB route this time." (Composite entry.)

"Pre-experiencing for me made possible no struggle at all when I got to the fork in the road (ice cream in my refrigerator). It was as if I had already taken charge of my inner choice, so there was no feeling of needing to gobble down food. The battle had already been fought in my bedroom away from the food earlier in the day— when I closed my eyes and imagined myself going through the day meeting those crossroads and going in my non-SDB direction and feeling good about it. Then I realized that when I used to set myself up for a battle at the fridge, I had already decided to lose the battle, or I wouldn't even be there dishing up the ice cream while fighting with myself or making all those 'I shouldn't do this' statements. Then I thought, 'Who's in charge of buying that ice cream in the first place?' I was! Wow! This is a revelation." (Composite entry.)

(From a thirty-one-year-old single male working on lack of confidence in relating to the opposite sex): "I made the inner decision not to marry. I also made an inner decision to not be completely responsible for my acts, especially in financial matters.... I must make an inner decision to marry and risk family life. I must make an inner decision to like myself with all my good qualities and my faults.... I must make an inner decision to be completely responsible for myself financially and not depend on my mother. I must make an inner decision to risk failure in all I do in order to be able to be a success and have the ability to pick myself up and keep going."(By permission.)

Let me here relate in summary a typical story that points out how we make these choices to get the SDB done. This defeating behavior pattern, although concerning a person working on weight, is somewhat common in all of us. It would be helpful to keep the road map in mind while following the story.

This participant told me she had serious overweight problems. She would get up on a beautiful day and decide, the first thing, to look at an illustrated cook book. (Most people would look outside or begin the morning chores, but this lady looked at a cook book.) Now, her inner choice is to bake a chocolate cake and eat the whole thing, but she does not admit such a thing to herself; and if you were to tell her that is what her goal is, she would indignantly deny it and become very angry at you for even suggesting such a thing. Looking at the cook book is her first choice in the outer choice area toward fulfilling her inner choice. Even as she gazes at the book she is telling herself that looking at pictures of cakes does not put on weight; that is a scientifically known fact.

She then discovers (of all things) a picture of a delicious chocolate cake. (Imagine that, right there in the cake section!)

After a few moments of vicarious imagining, she stops herself short with the thought, "But I'm on a diet. I can't have chocolate cake!"

So for a few moments she takes control and switches paths from her SDB to her non-SDB track. But that inner choice is still beckoning to bake and eat, and that choice is not on the non-SDB track. How is she going to switch back? That's easy—disown responsibility for it, and quickly minimize the prices.

This is how she did it: a few moments later the most interesting thought popped into her head. "What if company unexpectedly drops in? I don't have a thing in the house to offer them. Let's see now, what should I make?" (We already know, don't we?) So she decides to bake that chocolate cake for company. ("Company made me do it.")

Then she switches back again to her SDB route by getting the ingredients and going through all the outer choices and movements that are required to get a chocolate cake baked and frosted, any one of which, if not done, would prevent the chocolate cake from materializing: if she never stirred the ingredients, if she never put it in the oven or cake pan, if she never turned the oven on or took the cake out later. Check points all along the way could have stopped her.

Now she has developed the situation. There is the chocolate cake sitting on the cupboard looking extremely tempting and inviting; the day is practically gone (it's 10:00 a.m.), and company hasn't come yet (in fact, no one has been around for several days).

How to get that delicious cake inside her is now the problem. Rising to the self-created situation, she gets another flash of inspiration. "What if I offered some to company, and it was a bad cake!" (She also knows there is not such a thing as a bad chocolate cake, no matter how dry or how gooey.) So the only way to find out is to test it; and the only way to test it is to try a piece. At this point she has reached the fork in the road and is mentally and physically on her way to doing the SDB and paying the price. She minimizes here by telling herself one piece isn't going to make that much difference; there is still enough left for company.

When more than half the cake is consumed, she reaches a point of no return, and she recognizes and uses one truth: "Company isn't likely to come," and then another truth: "I've blown my diet for today." Then she decides: "I'll start again tomorrow, and, since I've gone this far and since I'm going to start tomorrow, I might as well eat the rest of it." So she does—just in time to hide the evidence before her husband comes home from work. Having used her SDB again, she begins to pay all the prices that have been patiently waiting at the end of the SDB route to be paid.

She feels very guilty and defensively snaps at her husband over trivia, feeling that he doesn't, even couldn't, love her anymore because of her weight—in spite of his efforts to let her know he does. She convinces herself she's no good and she's unworthy of anything coming her way—that surely she is despised. Her clothes continue not to look as nice as she would like, and standing before or even getting quick glimpses of herself in the mirror is depressing. And depression is the next round into which she slumps. (Modified and used by permission).

You will note many option points at which she could have taken control: looking at the cook book, mixing the ingredients, taking the first bite. If at any one of these points she had chosen to take control, it would not have ended the way it did.

Can you see *your* SDB pattern on this road map?

Can you recognize that the inner choice is very important but that it is not the *only* check point at which alternatives can be exercised?

A smoker who was trying to give up the habit discovered there were many check points along the SDB route that he could use to help himself. Each one could serve as a cue, like a warning signal on a highway, to alert him to the direction he was taking. Reaching into his pocket for the pack is one cue. If he did not do that small movement, the cigarette could not get into his mouth. If he *did* do that movement, taking the pack out of the pocket was another check point at which he could stop himself. Other points were flipping one cigarette out of the pack, taking it out, putting it into his mouth, holding it between his lips or teeth, putting the pack back into his pocket, reaching for the lighter or match, lighting the lighter or match, holding the flame at the end of the cigarette, inhaling through the cigarette, dousing the match or lighter, putting the lighter back into the pocket or throwing the match away, and sucking on the cigarette. All these are observable movements, and when any one of them is not done, the act of smoking cannot be accomplished. These movements, like driving a car, are done automatically, but they can be taken off "automatic pilot" and handled consciously in this effort to take control. Each movement also represents a second of time in which a new choice can be made to go either on the SDB or on the non-SDB route. Taking control in these outer-choice areas may be easier for some than taking control over the inner choice—or urge—that sets these movements into action. Some have found it possible to use the urge to light up another cigarette as a cue to trigger off alternative, nonsmoking behaviors in order to get on the non-SDB route.

Remember, the closer you come to doing the SDB, the harder it is to switch to the non-SDB route in that behavior cycle. There will always be alternatives in each of life's situations along the road of life, and as long as you have life in you, you are still able to exercise your agency to choose between the alternatives before you. (Chamberlain, 1976:40.)

STEP FOUR SUMMARY FORM: THE CHOICES I MAKE TO ACTIVATE MY SDB   DATE_____

I. The Inner Choices:
The inner choice or choices I have been making to activate

Alternative or non-SDB inner choice(s) I *should* make: (Ex.: "I will choose to eat sensibly

83

my SDB: (Ex.: "I have been choosing to bake a chocolate cake and eat the whole thing.")

and only what my body needs. I will choose to think of and do other things to occupy my time.")

_____
_____
_____
_____
_____

_____
_____
_____
_____
_____

II. The Outer Choices:
The outer choices I have been making to help carry out my inner choices: (Ex.: Look in cook book, bake it for company, put ingredients together, taste it.)

Alternative non-SDB choices I could make to support the non-SDB inner choices above: (Ex.: Clean house, think of my goals or plans, read, visit a wise friend.)

_____
_____
_____
_____

_____
_____
_____
_____

Critique for Step Four

Now look at your Step Four summary form. You should have written on it the inner and outer choices you make to keep your self-defeating behavior going. Do not make this a bigger chore than it is. It is simply writing down the choices you have been making that contribute to the result—your SDB—each time you do it. You can always tell what your inner choice was by the goal you reach in each behavior cycle. You will not reach that goal by chance.

Also, it is important to list the alternative choices open to you at any fork in the road. Your task is then to choose one or more of those alternative directions in a new moment of time to avoid the SDB route.

The following example from the summary form of a person with the SDB of excessive worry may help here. Don't forget to critique and make new comments on your diary entries since the last time. With this new information you can go back over your diary and, whenever possible, point out the choices you have made and how you have tended to shift the responsibility to others.

STEP FOUR SUMMARY FORM: THE CHOICES I MAKE TO ACTIVATE MY SDB   DATE March 6

(SDB: *Excessive Worry*)

Inner Choices:

The inner choice or choices I have been making to activate my SDB: (Ex.: "I have been choosing to bake a chocolate cake and eat the whole thing.")

I have been choosing to worry over past and future events over which I have no control. I have been choosing to worry about what everyone else is thinking. I have been choosing to make myself sick with worry.

Alternative or non-SDB inner choice(s) I should make: (Ex.: "I will choose to eat sensibly and only what my body needs. I will choose to think of and do other things to occupy my time.")

I choose to think of the positive here and now and to remind myself of my new label. I choose to look at what I can change and leave the rest to someone else. I choose to have a healthy mind and body. I choose to take the best action to solve a problem and forget about the rest.

The Outer Choices:

Outer Choices I have been making to help carry out my inner choice are: (Ex.: Look in cookbook, bake it for company, put ingredients together, taste it.)

Think about past mistakes at night. Concern myself with other SDBs. Dwell on what "might have been." Always look for and expect the worst possible thing to happen. Feel sorry for myself. Assume that I know what others are thinking. Sit and think myself into nonaction.

Alternative non-SDB choices I could make to support the non-SDB inner choices above: (Ex.: Clean house, think of my goals or plans, read, visit a wise friend.)

Choose to let the past go and take positive action in the present. To sleep at night knowing I have done my best. Look for the good and the positive. Allow others to have their own SDBs. Accept that I cannot solve all the world's problems.

(Composite entries.)

DAILY DIARY (SDB: *Inferiority feelings and shyness around girls*) Sept. 21

Briefly describe current experiences, feelings, thoughts, reactions, and actions that are in some way related to the self-defeating behavior you are trying to eliminate.

My Critique

I seem to be doing better. Last night at our young-adult church fireside, I saw this girl I had seen before. She was talking to a friend of hers, and I wanted so much to ask her for a date; but when I thought of doing it, I thought, "She probably already has a boyfriend, so I'd better not interfere." This choice would keep me from trying. I told myself, "You'll never know unless you find out by talking to her and asking her." I started to walk toward her and felt all my courage and resolution drain out of me as I came closer to where she was. She did not see me yet, and I kept telling myself I could still walk on past her and try again some other time when it was more convenient. Besides, my knees were beginning to shake and I felt wobbly and unsteady. What if I fell on the floor right in front of her? That would really make a big hit! Then I remembered my SDB road, the prices at the end—more lonely nights. I decided to stop a moment, get my breath, and see myself being friendly, like pre-experiencing the scene before it happened. Well, it worked! I got myself under control and had a good conversation with her and got a date! (Composite diary.)

I am improving and making progress when I put my mind to it.

I allow, by my own choices, negative thoughts to come in to keep me doing my SDB. Great! I caught that one. Good thinking!

I focused so much on *me*, that I scared myself almost into a panic to have an excuse for not trying. Chicken!

I really got my old adrenalin going that time. What I won't do to scare myself into my SDB route!

I *can* take control when I decide to. Wow! Keep it up!

DAILY DIARY (SDB: *Lack of motivation at college*) Nov. 7

Briefly describe current experiences, feelings, thoughts, reactions, and actions that are in some way related to the self-defeating behavior you are trying to eliminate.

I went to bed late last night because I was talking to my friends; so I didn't get up at 6:00 a.m. as I had planned, and I didn't study in the morning before class. In fact I was late getting to my second class and missed the first one completely. Then I went to the store instead of studying as my schedule required. I missed my language class because I did not feel I had time to go to it, and besides, I didn't have the work done for it. I don't like it and usually fall asleep in it.

I washed my clothes at the laundromat and felt tired and sick as I read magazines there waiting to get my clothes done. I didn't follow my schedule then either. But I did go and do some exercises at the gym and finally went back to the library to study. I got less than one hour of studying done, with many interruptions to look at girls going by my table near the entrance. I will follow my schedule. I am motivated. I love to study. I will get caught up. I will achieve my goals. I will go to bed now as it is time and on schedule.

11-8

I got up later than I should have. I was late for my first class. I scheduled things too close with no time to eat breakfast and get to class. I ate lunch on schedule, but I felt tired and sleepy after eating and felt a cold coming on. So I skipped language class again and slept an hour or two and missed some more classes. I felt better; so I worked over my schedule and plans and went to study at the library. By then it was 7:30. When I got there, I started to study and remembered the phone calls I wanted

I chose to stay up late and talk rather than go to bed to have this as a reason for not getting up early. It worked.

I chose to goof off at the store to keep myself from studying. Neat trick.

I chose not to get prepared for the language class in order to feel OK about not going to the class so that I could miss out on new assignments and get further behind. I make myself feel depressed and sick by these methods so that just living seems a drag. I tell myself I will do all these good things, but I know deep down inside that I have no intention of carrying through with them.

Who am I kidding? I do not value doing them. I do only what I value doing, no more nor less than that. I choose a time when I "should" get up, then I choose to fight against my own time schedule. Who am I disobeying, my parents? But they are not here now. I made certain I was late for class to convince myself how bad off I really am and how much I don't want to be

to make; so I spent most of the time in the
phone booth. I went to bed later than I
planned to. I am motivated. I will follow my
schedule. I am improving. I will continue.

11-9

I overslept this morning and felt sick with
a cold and a bad sore throat. So I got up
to eat lunch, went to the campus shop and
bought some things, and went to the ticket
place and bought tickets for my weekend
date. I didn't follow my schedule as I was
supposed to. I read papers and magazines
and another novel instead of information I
needed for my homework. I took a walk
and came back in time to eat and read
some more in that book. I talked with a girl
when I went out to do some visiting and
stayed late and didn't study. I went to bed
late. I will follow my schedule. I am
motivated. I wore a rock in my shoe all day
to remind me of my new label.

there anyway. I used my
"cold" trick to get me out of
classes, but did you notice I
did do the other things I
wanted to do? Who am I
kidding? I have my ways of
making myself feel miserable
and down on myself. They
worked. I chose to stay in
bed and tell myself my
throat was too bad, and it
caused me to stay in bed.
Yet I got other things done I
value doing.

11-10

Today I made it to two classes and
exercised but did not follow my homework
schedule at all. I didn't get to bed on time
last night, and I feel discouraged today. It is
all my fault. I am motivated as much as I
want to be. I must remember why I am
here at school. I must not rationalize away
my problems or procrastinate following
through. I can and will change now. I am
motivated. I will get caught up!

I make choices all along
during the day that keep me
in hot water with myself and
my school work. I am totally
in charge of these things. I
decided to stay out late so I
could not get my studies
done. It worked. I even like
to punish myself with this
rock in my shoe, but all I
seem to get out of it is a
sore foot. No matter how
much I tell myself these
positive things, nothing will
be different until I take
charge of the moments of
time, such as when it is time
to get up. I build myself up
to getting discouraged by all
the negative inputs I use to

_____

_____

_____

_____

_____

_____

_____

_____

11-19

Last night I didn't follow my schedule, and I had water balloon fights with the guys in the room next door. I stayed up late and didn't get to study for a test in my economics class. I was too tired, so I went to bed. I overslept and missed the economics and language classes. But I cleaned my room, hung up my clothes, wrote letters, and worked on this assignment for ESDB. I must change my ways. I am motivated. I didn't get to bed on schedule. I will set my schedule for tomorrow. I will make my schedule work for me. I will get caught up in school.
(By permission.)

keep my SDB going. I could choose to make non-SDB choices in these moments of living. I cannot keep telling myself I am on the non-SDB route, then do all that it takes to keep myself off it. I can choose in hard moments to sacrifice some fun and do what it takes to put myself on the non-SDB route. I have what it takes in me but I have been choosing not to use it yet. I chose to oversleep so that I could miss the test. In this way I can avoid unpleasant or difficult things. Do I get a grade for a clean room? No! Whose schedule do I think I am following? It is certainly not the one *I* made out. Do I make good-sounding schedules so that I can fight against them? Did I pay good money to come to college to skip classes and sleep as long as I want to?

Not unless I *do* it will I get caught up. Action must go with these words, or they are idle words and only make me feel more guilty.

Reference Notes:

1. Cudney, Milton R.
   1971 Elimination of Self-Defeating Behavior. Unpublished paper, Western Michigan University, Kalamazoo, Michigan.

References:

Chamberlain, Jonathan M.
   1976 Eliminating a Self-Defeating Behavior. Handbook for Education 514Rx-1, a Brigham Young University Home Study course: How to Eliminate a Self-Defeating Behavior: Brigham Young University Printing Services, Provo, Utah. Fourth edition.

STEP FIVE:
WHAT NEGATIVE TECHNIQUES DO I USE TO ACTIVATE MY SELF-DEFEATING CHOICES?

The plot thickens in this real-life drama to conquer your SDB. Hopefully by now you have been able to catch yourself making the inner and outer choices to do your SDB again. You are right on course if you have been able to catch that precious moment of choice and even better prepared to go on if you have been able to take control over it and make non-SDB choices and carry them out.

If you have been able to recognize that you are the chooser and the doer of your SDB, that is progress too. Having come this far, you have likely discovered there are certain ways of thinking that could be SDBs in themselves and that seem to contribute to your making SDB choices. These subtle "aids" to the accomplishment of your SDB we call *negative techniques.*

YOUR OBJECTIVES FOR STEP FIVE

You will be able to:
1. Identify and write the negative techniques you use to activate your SDB choices.
2. Recognize and write some positive techniques you need to develop and use to keep you on the non-SDB route.
3. Stop using the negative techniques that activate the SDB choices.

HOW TO PROCEED

To help you discover what your negative techniques are and how to control them, follow these procedures:
1. Read (1) "What Negative Techniques Do I Use to Activate Choices to Keep My SDB Going?" (2) "Sneaky Techniques" and (3) "Positive Techniques I Can Use" (following). Be sure to complete each assignment as it is given.

2. The written requirements for Step Five are to complete summary forms A and B and keep your daily diary for several more days.
3. When you have satisfied these requirements and have critiqued your work, you may go on to Step Six.

What Negative Techniques Do I Use to Activate Choices to Keep My SDB Going?

Remember, your self-defeating behaviors originate at a time of stress, anxiety, or fear. They are covering anxiety in such a way that you are convinced you cannot cope in life without them. At the time they were initiated, they seemed to be the only logical way to cope with the particular situation. Later they became self-defeating. They are kept going because you are afraid to face the fears you would feel if you did not use them; they are like a crutch. However, you pay deeply felt and very high prices to maintain them. You have learned also that the self-defeating behavior is not something you are but something you do and maintain, and in this way it is like a foreign object in your personal system. You sometimes use fears from the past to block off the nonself-defeating behavior road so that you continually go the self-defeating behavior route.

You learned in Step Four that you make five major choices to keep it going: (1) you choose to do your SDB: (2) you use outer choices to carry out inner decisions; (3) you choose to minimize the prices you pay for doing the self-defeating behavior; (4) you choose to become irresponsible and disowning long enough to do it again; and (5) you choose to abandon your best self each time you do it.

Subtle ways are needed to implement all these choices to make them seem more presentable to you so that you can justify doing them again. These ways are called techniques. Those that lead into the doing of a SDB are negative techniques.

Those that help you on the non-SDB route are positive techniques. Negative techniques are ways of thinking or things you do to help you decide to make defeating choices. Some examples of very commonly used negative techniques are comparing yourself to others, anticipating certain things to happen, distorting feedback, manipulating things and people to maintain the behavior, labeling yourself and others, intellectualizing, pouting, blanking your mind so that you can't deal with the problem effectively, and placing unrealistic expectations on yourself and on others. One that is perhaps overused by many is the technique of getting discouraged so that choosing to do an SDB is made easier.

From these examples you can see that these techniques are things you do as well as ways of thinking. They are the tools with which defeating-behavior patterns are built. Negative techniques are to a self-defeating behavior what fuel is to a fire—without something on which to burn, the fire would die out. Without techniques to keep it going, the self-defeating behavior would cease to exist. (Cudney, note 1.)

One participant stated, "My self-defeating behavior is like crabgrass roots intertwined and intermeshed into my whole life in the way I think and feel and the things I do, and this program is threatening to jerk all that out of me. It will leave a gaping hole." Let's think of it this way: crabgrass roots are identifiable and different from other roots. When you come to one, snip it off and pull it out. When you come to another one, snip it off and pull it out so that it will not feed into the main plant. The last one is just one more snip—not a gaping hole. This breaks down the behavior in such a way that it is manageable. When you control the techniques you use to feed the self-defeating behavior, you have practically won the battle.

Taking over control of the negative techniques you use is like starving the SDB at its roots or like turning off the fuel supply to the fire you have kept going. It becomes an extremely simple thing to do and very effective. But you must not let the simplicity of it scare you into making it harder to give up than it really is.

Some people go to great lengths to use new techniques when old ones become inoperable because of the owners' total awareness of them.

The object of this step is to help you discover the negative techniques you use and to help you stop using them, to discover and develop the use of some positive techniques to help you avoid using the negative ones, and to help you stay on the non-SDB route. In most cases, when this is accomplished it will make the doing of the SDB impossible. There may be some fears attached to doing without the self-defeating behavior; however, using fears is only another negative technique to help keep the behavior going. When you convince yourself you cannot do without the SDB because of the fear, realize what you are doing and how you use fear to frighten you out of changing. Further help in facing what fears you may have will be given you in Step Six. But you will be more ready and able to do Step Six if you have completed Step Five first.

Some negative techniques are easily detected; others are more subtle, hidden within the inner world of your thinking. Many have to do with your ways of thinking that allow you to make all the choices needed to do the self-defeating behavior. You can identify all these techniques. Then you can and must choose to stop using them.

Sneaky Techniques

Negative techniques you use to help maintain your SDB are identifiable. Once they are identified, they stand out like the large road signs above the freeway that point to your SDB destination. They are in effect saying "SDB this way." You must then choose not to follow their direction. They lead only to your doing the SDB again and to those prices you do not want to pay any more.

As indicated above, control over your techniques makes the battle simple. You merely starve out the SDB so that it doesn't have a chance to exist any more. The old method of fighting against your SDB directly is like trying to stop a car coming at you sixty miles per hour—a car *you* had set in motion yourself farther back down the road. You are determined to stop it with your bare hands, but what usually happens is that you get overpowered and mashed against your price list.

Contrast the effort and time and pain inflicted upon yourself in this way with that of simply getting ahead of the problem and turning off the key to the car *before* it gets started down the SDB freeway. We sometimes set the SDB machinery into motion, then allow it to gain momentum. We realize the problem is bigger than we are, and we are convinced we are helpless to stop it. Taking charge of the technique you use is like draining the tank of its fuel supply so that even if you do turn the key on, the car will not get very far. When you recognize that you are in charge of setting it into motion, you can choose not to do it and spare yourself a lot of trouble later on. Remember, you can never do an SDB without paying the prices attached. They will be paid. They are found on the SDB road much like a toll fee that must be paid for going in that direction.

Some participants in this program exclaim, "Something must be wrong; it can't be that simple!" Some even feel scornful of themselves because they have discovered they had been trying to make it harder to change than they needed to. Some become fearful that they *will* change now that it has become so clear *how* to.

It is simple; yet do not doubt its effectiveness. Investing more thought and energy into techniques for controlling the inner choice will make almost unnecessary any investment of energy in a struggle to resist the SDB. The quiet battle will have already been fought in a prior moment of decision and commitment, and there will be no wavering or struggling against your SDB at the brink of temptation.

Of course, not everyone reacts to these basic principles in the same way. Do not allow yourself to feel discouraged if your experiences do not correspond precisely with those described in this book. You will have your unique experiences in applying these principles. Learn from them.

Some people experience a shifting from the SDB road to the non-SDB road, back and forth, until they are not certain which way they really want to go. Usually this self-imposed confusion is only a subtle negative technique to help keep the SDB going. It is like placing fog at the intersection on the road so that you can do the SDB undercover of the fog. Or, it is like a person who, working on giving up compulsive eating, "finds himself" standing by the refrigerator door with a piece of cake in one hand, pushing it away from his mouth with the other until he finally gets to the point that he can say in exasperation "Oh, what the heck! It's not worth the hassle." When you arrive at that point, which road do you usually take? You take the SDB route, and do it again. You can see that the intent of that type of "back and forth" behavior is to wear yourself down and get discouraged in order to feel justified in giving in to the SDB. You tease yourself along and set up the process to accomplish the SDB. The person in this illustration had already decided to eat the cake, or he would not have been there struggling not to until he finally gave in to his inner choice—made earlier. Sometimes we make up a mock or sham battle in an attempt to convince ourselves and perhaps others how *truly hard* we are trying to lick this problem.

It is always harder to fight the enemy in his territory than in your own, and you have compounded the difficulty to fight it on the SDB roadway at a point of no return. You may go down in heroic defeat, but the whole battle was in vain and needless.

Many discover how they have been using *comparing* as a negative technique to make them feel bad about themselves, or, on the other hand, to convince themselves they need not change anything. Here is the way that one seems to work against you. When you compare yourself negatively in some way to someone else, whether you end on top of the comparison or on the bottom, the comparison serves the same purpose—to keep your SDB going. When you find yourself on the bottom of a comparison, you do it usually to make yourself feel low, dumb, or worthless. This feeling allows you to put into operation those choices needed to maintain the SDB. If, on the other hand, you place yourself on top in a comparison, you are usually patting yourself on the back because you are not as bad off as that poor fellow, and you can justify no need for change so that you can keep the SDB going. On the one hand, you decide change is hopeless or that the struggle is useless; on the other, you decide change is not necessary. Either position brings the same result—you continue to do the SDB involved. Notice how very carefully you select the "right" person to compare yourself with so as to get the results you want in order to keep the SDB going.

Impatience is another common technique. It seems to serve no other purpose than to help maintain your SDB choices. Remember that in this business you cannot afford to be impatient. It takes time to work out your problems, and you have all the time it takes.

Fear is another one. When you examine fear closely, you will find that it is totally within yourself and that you use it generally to maintain the SDB pattern. Step Six will deal more specifically with fear and its role in your pattern of behavior.

If you find at this point in the program that you are allowing yourself to fear what will happen when you truly drop your SDB, that fear is "right on" for now. But you need not let that feeling dictate your behavior now that you can recognize it as a very subtle (should I say *sneaky?*) technique to help you keep your SDB pattern going.

If you can frighten yourself with enough anxious feelings to drop the program at this point, you have defeated the program in an obvious attempt to hang on to the behaviors that have hurt you so much.

Discouragement seems to be a major negative technique. It is almost the main line leading to making SDB choices. Whatever you do or think to achieve the feeling of discouragement, whether it be comparing, impatience, or unrealistic expectations, you can rest assured that your thoughts and actions are aimed at helping you do the SDB. I can think of no better purpose for discouragement than to keep a self-defeating behavior alive and happy. But fortunately *you can actually decide not to let yourself feel discouraged!* You are also in charge of your moods and attitudes.

Let me give you a few examples of how others have used negative techniques to keep the SDB going:

"I assumed I knew what others were thinking; but those were really my thoughts, not theirs, and of course I assumed the worst. Then I reacted to them as if they were really thinking that about me. They had no other choice than to confirm my suspicions. I had set a trap, and they had fallen into it; and I told myself, 'They can't be trusted.' My assuming what others were thinking about me was a technique that set me up for trouble."

"If I could get my wife angry at me, I had a perfectly good excuse to make my SDB choice to do it again." (This man used his wife's anger as a technique to set off his choices to activate his SDB pattern.) (Composite entries.)

Before reading any further in this area, stop now and list some of the negative techniques you have been using to activate your SDB choices. You may write these on the Step Five Summary Form A provided for this purpose, or make your own form on a separate sheet of paper. After you have written all the negative techniques you can discover, read over the list provided on the next few pages to see if some additional ones belong to you. You might wish to add them to your own list so that you can expose them for what they really are and begin to avoid using them because they set you up for your SDB.

You will notice that some of them are SDBs in themselves but are used as supporting techniques for other SDBs. For example, some people have used homosexual behavior to support fear of the opposite sex and fear of risking marriage. When they discovered that this behavior was only a technique, these individuals were able to face their fear more squarely; they were able to date people of the opposite sex and eventually to marry. If your inner choice is to remain single, techniques and choices are necessary to bring about that result.

STEP FIVE SUMMARY FORM A: NEGATIVE TECHNIQUES I USE TO ACTIVATE MY SDB CHOICES   DATE_____

The negative techniques I use, or have used, to activate my SDB choices are as follows:

_____

_____

_____

_____

_____

_____

_____

_____

_____

_____

Some Typical Negative Techniques

The following list of negative techniques is by no means an all-inclusive one. The examples are numerous, however, and characteristic of those people often use. Study over the list of techniques and check the ones you use. Remember that in order to maintain self-defeating behavior patterns, negative techniques are required. If you identify these and make a commitment to stop them, you will stand face to face with the fears from which the techniques have helped you run. The opportunity will then be yours to free yourself from your SDB.

- To agree with people on the surface when you do not agree inside.
- To avoid the unknown by not speaking unless you are sure ahead of time exactly what you are going to say.
- To make other people's reactions so important they override your own beliefs.
- To respond to life in a feelingless manner and to avoid emotionally laden subjects.
- To hang onto old familiar ways of responding because it seems safer.
- To take a test such as an interest or personality test and to give the test power over your own decisions.
- To put unrealistic expectations on yourself or others.

- To use an "I am" label (as "an alcoholic," for example) and by so doing view yourself as having a condition, then to use this as a subtle means for shifting the responsibility for what you do onto that condition, or convincing yourself that is what you *are* instead of what you *do*.
- To *do* homosexuality but to use an *I am* label by considering yourself as *being* a homosexual and believing there is no sense trying to fight what you are.
- To hold onto a poor concept, comparing yourself to others and coming off second-best all the time. (You carefully select the "right" person to make this happen.)
- To keep from venturing into the unknown by bringing previous defeats into your mind.
- To lump people into categories and to react to them according to the way you lumped them rather than as the unique individuals they are.
- To institutionalize deviant sexual behavior by developing views that society is an ogre for not accepting this behavior as normal, by involving self in the gay and loose liberation movements, and by surrounding yourself with people who reinforce these behaviors.
- To be argumentative as a way of not getting into deeper issues.
- To misuse drugs, but to become an expert at identifying society's faults.
- To build a deceptive wall around yourself so that no one can get near, then to refer to this defensiveness as *depth* and to try to convince yourself and others that this so-called depth is a mark of distinction. (People are often able to elicit praise for this "depth.")
- To break up relationships as a way of not having to build close and lasting ones, but to make it appear that the other person is at fault.
- To go about doing weird things as a way to keep convincing yourself how terrible you are.
- To begin a lot of tasks but not to finish them.
- To blank your mind when you are getting close to important data.
- To imagine what other people are thinking and feeling rather than to check out reality. To project your own meaning onto another's intentions and to react as if they were really the other person's thoughts.

- To know something important is going on in yourself but to keep it vague.
- To avoid eye contact and to develop various looks that communicate to other people how shy you are so that they will stay away.
- To turn caring on and off, depending upon how close another person gets to covered data.
- To take something that was not really a problem in the past (such as being an adopted child) and to make it a problem to cover up facing something in the present (such as loneliness or nontrusting).
- To lie.
- In interactions with other people, to give them only partial data about yourself so that they cannot know who you really are.
- To take something someone else says, often words of an expert, and to make a rule out of that for yourself so that you do not have to trust yourself.
- To keep so busy there is little time or energy left to think about yourself or to face deep issues.
- To use denseness or confusion as a way of not understanding information and concepts that might lead you to face fears.
- To pick out something someone else does that really is a mistake and to add to this mistake while putting the total responsibility onto the other person.
- To cry as a way of not having to face deeper issues.
- To hold honest crying back as a means of not expressing feelings.
- To minimize the good aspects of life and to overexaggerate mistakes and bad points.
- To "make a mountain out of a molehill."
- To distort praise and to minimize other people's feedback.
- To take direction for what you ought to do in many of life's situations from sources outside yourself, but to do it in such a way that you do not have to trust yourself. These other sources can be other people (especially experts), books, religious doctrines, and magic.
- To have a real and strong feeling but to keep it longer than is necessary and fitting.
- To take something that is valid (like tiredness or a real limitation) and to magnify it in such a way as to incapacitate yourself.

- When faced with a conflict, to build added tension and to involve yourself with the tension to avoid the real conflict.
- To rationalize that someone won't like you as a means of not checking out the reality of that thought.
- To maintain the idea that it is weak and wrong to ask for help and to believe you ought to be able to work out your own difficulties, even when your reality says differently.
- To maintain guilt about "water over the dam" that you cannot do anything about.
- To take a reality (such as a spouse's sex interest) and to perceive it as something dirty, as gluttonous, and as an excessive demand.
- To maintain an erroneous positive perception about yourself, such as "I am honest" as a means of being able to overlook your dishonest acts.
- To know how to respond to a situation but to convince yourself otherwise.
- To maintain the attitude that life is a game with all the rules of a game. (By so doing you never have to respond honestly.)
- To not like the way another person responds and to use it as an excuse for not having to change something inside yourself.
- When someone touches a reality about you, especially if it is unpleasant, to deny that it hit home.
- To take on a lot of little tasks to the point of immobilizing yourself by not choosing what is important and unimportant in life. (Never saying no to others helps you accomplish this.)
- To believe the problem is outside of you when, in fact, it is inside—or vice versa.
- To pick friends, or a spouse, who will reinforce your SDBs.
- To make people as objects in your mind, then to manipulate them, as needed, to let yourself remain stagnant.
- To see the SDB pattern manifested in only one situation, i.e., with your girl friend, but to ignore its emergence and use in other situations.
- To openly admit using one or more techniques but to do it in such a way that you do not have to change it.
- To create an outer restrictive box and then to see the box (now with people in it, such as a boss or spouse or parents) as not allowing you to move very much.

- Not to demand certain things you have a right to demand.
- To tell yourself you have nothing in common with anyone else and, therefore, nothing to talk about.
- To not know what someone else is going to say but to brace yourself against it anyway.
- To forget selectively (to choose what to forget).
- To appear sleepy.
- To exaggerate a truth.
- To put on an air of hostility and then, with a scowl and a chip on the shoulder, to keep others away.
- To cut yourself down before others do.
- To distract yourself when doing an important task like studying.
- To maintain inappropriate silence.
- To "computerize" responses rather than to give fresh responses to fresh situations.
- To bend your feelings.
- To set up a situation a day ahead of time that will defeat you but then to disown setting it up and to see the situation as at fault.
- To predict what situations will be like, to get ready for the predictions, and never to take life as it comes.
- To avoid taking care of your appearance or body or room as a way of convincing yourself you need to be taken care of. (People often will work at making their financial situation a shambles for the very same reason.)
- To do a lot of irresponsible things but to perceive them as a mark of freedom.
- To look dumb.
- To worry about problems that cannot be changed.
- To try to talk over other people's heads.
- To go into a classroom situation with the attitude that the total responsibility for getting anything out of the class is all on the instructor's shoulders.
- To maintain a variety of "voices" designed to manipulate others and to keep a SDB pattern. (The voices can be used to communicate dependency, helplessness, harshness, pathos, and so forth, and can vary from a whine to an ultra-powerful sound.)
- To know what you must do in a given situation but not to trust your own knowledge and to ask another person for advice in order to escape the responsibility for a mistake.

- Not to know the answers to real problems but not to use your own thinking processes in searching for answers or to pretend you already know so that you can keep yourself from learning. (Adapted from Cudney, 1975:46-51.)

Positive Techniques I Can Use

Up to now we have been concerned with your recognizing the negative techniques you use to help you make your SDB choices. Now begin to think about some of the positive techniques you need to use, or perhaps have already begun to use, to help keep you on the *non-SDB* route. At first these may seem very few, but as you commit yourself to stay on the non-SDB route, you will find many ways to help you remain on that best-self course.

Here are a few examples of how others have developed *positive techniques* to help keep them on the non-SDB route:

"When I was tempted to switch back to my SDB track, I would imagine my disgusting price list waiting there to be paid, and I would tell myself: 'I'm not going to be robbed by them anymore!'"

"I tell myself, 'I don't need to do this SDB anymore.'"

"I started going with friends who did not do my SDB and soon learned to feel just as great with them as I did with my SDB friends—but without the price tags."

"I used my price list to block the SDB road so that I had to see what it cost me before I went in that direction." (Composite entries.)

Take some time to write down a list of the positive techniques you can or should develop to help you divert your old pattern onto the non-SDB route. The Step Five Summary Form B is designed for this purpose.

Below are some additional examples of positive techniques to help you.

- Deciding to make new friends who do not reinforce my SDB pattern.
- Thinking of myself as a person with my own rights.
- Thinking "I have a right to be me without my SDB."
- Recognizing that others must accept me for whatever I am at my best self; and if they don't accept that, then it is *their* SDB, not mine.
- Deciding not to let others' SDBs become mine nor to assume the responsibility for their SDBs.
- Deciding to not allow myself to have feelings of discouragement, impatience, or depression, and if I am already depressed, to accept it and go on from there.

103

- Deciding to open up my thinking to allow myself to see other alternatives and to think of solutions to a problem.
- Sharing with others what changes I am trying to make so that I can elicit their help and make it an open commitment to change.
- Think over various aspects of this change program to help remind me of where and who I really am.
- Do helpful things for others to take the focus off myself, to help me be "turned out" rather than "turned in."

Remember that for you to follow the self-defeating road, you must use negative techniques to implement self-defeating choices. Remember also, SDBs do not happen on their own. *You* must *do* them if they are to survive.

On the other hand, when you follow the non-SDB route, you must make decisions to implement these life choices. Begin to make these life transactions consciously and then, with increasing awareness, follow them. In following the life road, your transactions eventually become very wide and very deep and you will discover new freedoms in various moments of living.

If you haven't already done so, complete Step Five now by implementing the following activities on the summary forms A and B:

First: study your behavior carefully and list the negative techniques you use, then look at the list provided in this book to gain some additional ones.

Second: Make your own list on Step Five Summary Form A (or on your own form).

Third: After you have made your list, add to it any other negative techniques you discover as you go along, so that you will be fully aware of all techniques you are using. Once you have listed your techniques, be on guard when you are about to use one of them again. Stop yourself and don't use it. Let yourself experience *you* at your best without the SDB. Face whatever fears or feelings you need to face at that moment, knowing that the fears are only feelings from within you and that life is always better without the self-defeating behavior.

Fourth: Begin to make a list on Summary Form B of *positive techniques* that will help you keep on the non-SDB route. Then *use* them.

Fifth: Critique your diary again, looking for choices and techniques.

STEP FIVE SUMMARY FORM B: POSITIVE TECHNIQUES I CAN USE TO SUPPORT MY NON-SDB CHOICES DATE___

Positive techniques I must develop to help keep myself on the non-SDB road (make this as specific as possible to fit your own behavior pattern):

_____
_____
_____
_____
_____
_____
_____
_____
_____
_____
_____
_____
_____
_____
_____
_____
_____
_____
_____
_____
_____
_____
_____
_____
_____
_____

Critique for Step Five

There is not much more you can do with your list on Summary Form A showing your negative techniques except to write in the right-hand margin these words or something like them: "Now that these techniques are exposed to me for what they really are, I will choose not to use them." "I will catch myself about to use any of these and will use my positive techniques in their place."

The following examples of these entries and a diary may help:

Negative Techniques I Use (Form A)	My Critique
• I assure myself that there is always tomorrow.	These are all irrational ways of thinking and doing and now that I have revealed them to be what they really are, I can spot them coming and choose not to use them.
• I block out my mind as to the consequences of my act.	
• I numb myself to guilt feelings about performing my SDB.	
• I tell myself I am not worth improving (self-depreciation).	Great going!
• I tell myself everyone is happy but me.	
• I "reward" my non-SDB behavior with my SDB.	See how clever you are.
• I tell myself that one slip or relapse ruins the whole program.	You know all the answers.
• I confuse the thought with the act and then feel that because I even considered doing my SDB, I might as well go all the way.	
• I tease my self-control to see how far I can withstand temptation.	All of these will help you stay on the non-SDB route!
• I mentally whip myself for past failures.	

Positive Techniques I Will Develop

• I will take one day at a time. I can't change anything tomorrow. I can only take charge over now and today.

• I will keep my price list handy and see and feel ahead of time what it is going to cost me to do it.

• I will avoid guilt feelings by being on top of things in the first place and not doing my SDB.

• I have innate personal power. What more could I ask? I deserve better treatment than this.

• I can focus on others rather than on

106

> myself, looking for the good in others,
> not the bad.
> * I will reward myself for not doing my
>   SDB by doing something self-enhancing,
>   not self-defeating.
> * I will let negative thoughts go and not let
>   them take root in my behavior.
> * I will pre-experience what is ahead on
>   both my SDB and my non-SDB routes,
>   then choose the results I want for myself.
> * I will let the past be and will live now and
>   plan for the future. I will stop looking
>   back at past failures. (Composite entries.)

DAILY DIARY (SDB: Depressed and Worthless Feelings)

Saturday

> I make weekends my worst time by
> having no deadline, no plans. I just let
> myself drift, and of course I tend to drift
> into my SDB. My mind plays havoc with me
> (I mean I let it). Although I have not let my
> SDB thoughts culminate in the act, I sure
> have been fighting a bloody mental battle.
> Sometimes if I can talk to myself out loud, I
> can talk myself out of the anxiety by
> reminding myself of the prices, choices, and
> techniques. I realize I am truly my own
> worst enemy. I am waging one last battle,
> and it's weird.

I can recognize now how *I* make things turn out for me.

I like to toy around with SDB thoughts to tease myself and make it harder for me to change.

I could choose to avoid the battle and not make it so "bloody" and difficult for me.

I am making progress, though I seem to have to make it an all-out battle instead of a quiet victory.

Sunday

> My days seem to follow a cycle. I usually
> start fresh in the morning with a "nothing's
> going to stop me" feeling. But I let it slide
> down hill from there so that by night time
> I'm plaguing myself with SDB thoughts. I
> haven't yet succumbed, but I feel mentally
> tired from wrestling with myself. Thank
> goodness I have tasted the exhilarating

I choose to feel stronger in the mornings and let myself do some drifting later on.

Of all the things in the world I choose to dwell upon, it is my SDB so that I can play the martyr role and make a big battle out of it.

feeling of self-control in the program so far	I can and will hang on. *I*
which makes it much harder to return to my	am succeeding!
SDB. A taste of victory is great!	

Monday	
It's strange how some days I can feel so	Do I hang on to the edge
strong while at other times it's all I can do	of the prices when I could
to keep from going under. It simply further	remove myself far from it?
supports the idea that my SDB is a lot	
more than mere "ripples" in a pond.	
There's a sort of seething, deep cauldron of	I am starting to scare
fear bubbling within me. It's scary and	myself so that I can use that
spooky!	feeling to help me keep my
	SDB.

Tuesday	
Lincoln stated that people are just about	
as happy as they decide to be. Well I've	Excellent spirit!
decided to smash this SDB and that's all	
there is to it. I really want to become a fully	
self-actualizing person. I realize that	
"improvement" starts with me. I've been	
very sharp at catching myself trying to reach	
into my magic bag of tricky techniques. And	
when I start to pull one out, I just laugh:	I am developing a way to
"Not on your life, Buster." It sounds crazy,	handle my old negative
but it works for now. And that's what	techniques!
counts. I am succeeding! (Printed by	
permission.)	

Reference Notes:

1. Cudney, Milton R.
   1971 Elimination of Self-Defeating Behavior. Unpublished paper. Western Michigan University, Kalamazoo, Michigan.

References:

Cudney, Milton R.
   1975 Eliminating Self-Defeating Behaviors. Kalamazoo, Michigan: Life Giving Enterprises.

STEP SIX:
WHAT FEARS MUST I FACE TO BE ME WITHOUT MY SDB?

YOUR OBJECTIVES FOR STEP SIX

You will be able to:

1. Identify and state the fears you may feel without your self-defeating behavior.
2. Recognize those fears as mythical in nature.
3. Indicate the positive benefits you will receive by dropping your SDB.

HOW TO PROCEED

In order to complete this step, read on, continue to write your daily diary, and complete forms A and B for Step Six. After making sure you have completed all the assignments and activities for this step, review and critique your work, then continue on to Step Seven.

What Fears Must I Face to Be Me Without My SDB?

You were born whole, without self-defeating behavior patterns. At birth and during infancy you responded as an integrated self to the world. As you grew up, you learned there are opposites and alternatives in life. You learned that two or more directions are open to you in each of life's situations. To the degree that your cultural circumstances did not accept and honor your integrated best self and warped the mirrors of those significant others from whom you incorporated information about yourself into your personal system, to that degree you took on self-defeating patterns in order to respond to your world. After your first encounter with an anxiety-producing incident, you had two ways of reacting: (1) to respond to your world as your fitting self on the non-SDB route, or (2) to abandon your fitting self and meet your world instead with the SDB patterns you had learned. (Adapted from Cudney, 1975.)

Meeting new moments of living with old SDB patterns requires a lot of effort and ingenuity on your part, like the effort required to carry around one or more wastepaper baskets. In addition to the five major choices already discussed in the previous steps, keeping your self-defeating behavior includes keeping fears from past experiences and using them in your present life moments in such a way that you can decide to abandon your integrated self.

You experienced a fear or an anxiety feeling in the past at the time of one incident or more that caused you to forsake your whole or integrated self in order to cope with that situation. For example, suppose that on your first day at school at age five you were full of enthusiasm, feeling absolutely on top of the world as you entered the classroom to start school; but your teacher had too many "exuberant scholars" and felt too short on patience with all of them. Before long you learned, in perhaps an embarrassing way, that being you at your best was not pleasing to her and that to remain there you had to please her. In order to do that, you had to abandon something of yourself to conform to her mood and to the situation. She may have singled you out as a "bad" person and made an example of you in front of the class. In that moment of embarrassment, perhaps you learned several erroneous ideas about yourself that were based on your level of understanding at the time. Some of those erroneous learnings may have been not to trust your own senses, or that school is a bad place to be, or that you have to fight teachers and authority figures like her to get along, or that you have to be someone you are not at school, or that it is best to be a frightened, quiet "mouse" in the classroom, or "I'm a bad person," or "I'm dumb." You could have adopted any or all of these learnings, and thus you have spent the rest of your life in or out of school upholding some erroneous self-image. Your whole life may have been colored by these traumatic earlier experiences. You may have put on a negative label that you upheld by your self-defeating behaviors since that childhood experience.

These erroneous conclusions about yourself are based on your perceptions at the time you were under stress, and were, therefore, deeply impressed learnings. Because you had no great store of knowledge or wisdom at that early age from which to draw for a better understanding of the situation, you likely misunderstood some of what was going on. The behavior that you gradually developed into a pattern and that became self-defeating to you was originally meant to cope with the stressful situation. Thus, in your present life, that behavior is based on fear—fear of reexperiencing that originally felt, but now stored away, embarrassed feeling.

Using this mental process, one person, who had concluded at the age of three that she was going to die of cancer because several people whom she loved—including her own mother—had died of cancer, had harbored a mysterious but real pain in her side for years until she became a participant in this program at forty-five, working to eliminate her fear of death. Another person had erroneously concluded at age three from an incident in her life that she was ugly and that boys had to be bested at intellectual things. She upheld both of these erroneous learnings until she faced these feelings. At age twenty-seven, single, she participated in this program to eliminate biting her fingernails (a "keeping myself ugly SDB"). Because the program was successful, she felt and became more attractive, dated a fine college student, married, and has two children at this writing. Later, upon completing the program a second time, she was successful in eliminating competitive feelings against her husband and other men.

A forty-year-old inmate at a state prison had erroneously concluded at the age of seven that he had killed his brother, who was six. Because of an accident on the street over which he had no control, he upheld a "bad boy" image through six marriages and divorces, bad checks, and alcoholism.

Another middle-aged man maintained a weight loss of over forty-five pounds after he discovered that he had erroneously concluded as a child in his high chair that he had to eat more than he could hold comfortably in order to please and be loved by his mother and grandmother, both of whom were there with full spoons, stuffing food into his mouth until *they* were satisfied he had eaten enough. His fear of being unloved by them had kept him eating too much.

If ridicule, or the fear of it, caused you initially to abandon yourself and use a SDB to cope with that fear, you will likely fear ridicule now as you consider reclaiming your best self by giving up your SDB. If being rejected led to your abandoning your best self in the past, you may fear rejection now as you decide to operate out of your fitting self again. If you concluded you must be a terrible person because of the warped messages you received from your culture or peers, you may likely fear finding a terrible person within and be unable to see the creative person you really are. SDBs are maintained partially by the fears held in the memory, planted there by erroneous conclusions in a time of stress or anxiety. There are many causes for the creation of SDB patterns. Once they are learned, however, there is one reason they are kept going. That is the fear of operating without them. You can ask yourself, "What is it I would be afraid to face if I did not use this SDB pattern to respond to my present world?" The fear is similar to that of a boy told to throw away his crutches after his leg has healed: "Will I be able to stand alone? Will I fall? Will it hurt?"

The fear of being without SDB patterns is stored in the memory banks within your human system. When you come to a new moment of living, you trigger off the stored fears from the past and project them down the non-SDB road. You thus close off the non-SDB road with these fears so that it seems too difficult to attempt. Also, you are temporarily more certain of the results on your SDB road because you have learned to count on suffering the consequences and paying the prices that always await there. The non-SDB road seems uncertain, and you frighten yourself with that uncertainty.

Before eliminating their defeating patterns, most people are convinced that the fears they feel inside are not mythical. They "swear" that if they follow their integrated selves without the SDB, what they fear will really happen. This is understandable because at the time the SDB was conceived the experiences were real, and the perception of that reality is stored in your memory. As soon as you admit that you are using these old stored-up fears in order to keep from following the integrated self, you can begin to see that the fears are a myth. But you may not be convinced until you go down the non-SDB road and meet these fears and work through them. This step prepares you to do that.

Before going further, search deeply within yourself and write on the Summary Form A for Step Six a list of all the things you fear, or are concerned·about, or feel worried over, that are in some way related to giving up your SDB. After making your list, you may review on the following pages some examples from others to help you add to your list. Note that there are two parts on form A and a form B to complete for this step.

Listing My Fears

Do not concern yourself if the "fear" categories seem to get mixed up with each other. The important thing is to get out into the open all the fears you may be harboring regarding giving up the self-defeating behavior on which you have been working.

112

If you have been able to rid yourself of the SDB before now and feel no fears about its absence, so much the better. Some participants are able to do this. You may wish, then, to state what your fears used to be or to state your current feelings about giving up the SDB.

If you are still doing your SDB but feel no fears about giving it up, perhaps you could investigate more thoroughly the reasons why you don't stop doing something you have determined is defeating to you. Think this through carefully.

Writing these fears on the Summary Form A for this step where you can see them and think them through helps to reduce them to manageable size and helps you to recognize them as threats you carry within yourself and, therefore, as mythical fears that have dictated your behavior in the past.

Following are three categories of fears people use to keep their SDB patterns going:

Category 1: **Some people fear they will not like their integrated selves if they let the SDBs go.**
- I will find out I am a person I couldn't like.
- I will be dumb and incompetent after all.
- I won't have warmth to communicate. I'll be cold and unfeeling.
- I will be weak and vulnerable.
- I will not be up to the task of coping with life.
- I will be inadequate—verbally, intellectually, emotionally, and physically.
- I will find I have no inner self. I am afraid I will find my entire self is full of SDBs.
- I will find a person full of hate.
- I will find an untrustworthy person.
- I will be unattractive.
- I will be unable to control my emotions: anger, sadness, loneliness, happiness.
- I will find a sex maniac within myself.
- I will find a person lacking in common sense.
- I will find a person unable to handle responsibility.
- I will find a person unable to change.
- I will find out I am a hideous person.
- I will find a mentally ill person.
- I will be frigid.
- I will be incompatible with the rest of society.
- I will find a conformist.

- I will be lazy.
- I will find a person who likes being bad.

Category 2: Some people fear they will become too vulnerable if they do not use their SDB patterns.
- Others will lose respect for me and will disapprove and reject me.
- I fear that if I drop my SDBs, I will hurt so much over what I have done in the past I won't be able to handle it.
- I fear I will lose the security I now have.
- Demands will be put on me I can't handle.
- If others do not want me around, I will be so lonely I will not be able to cope with it.
- I will be terribly hurt if I do not hold myself back.
- Someone will see my true feelings and take advantage of me.
- Responsible living will be too heavy, and I will not like it or be able to cope with it satisfactorily.
- I will do things to drive away people who are important to me.
- I will be stuck with whom I find and will be unable to change.
- God will condemn me.
- I will mess up the future.
- I will be caught forever in deep depressions with no way to get out.
- I will look foolish.
- I won't be able to control my own time.
- I will have no control over wrong things I will say.
- People will ridicule me, and I will have no satisfactory way to handle this.
- I fear I will die a horrible death.
- I will be lost forever.
- I will be shut away in an institution.
- I do not know what will happen, but I fear it will be bad.
- Unknowingly I will damage others.
- It will disturb my family relationships too much.

Category 3: Some people will have generalized fears about going down the non-SDB road.
- I fear the non-SDB route will be more difficult than the defeating route.
- The non-SDB route is more risky than the defeating one.

- **I'll have to pay even higher prices to give up my SDB pattern. (Cudney, 1975:21-23.)**

Fears, Fears

The following is a story told by a person attempting to overcome a SDB. "The mythical fear and the way we avoid facing it by doing our SDB reminds me of when I was about twelve years old and served as a babysitter to my married sister's children. Late at night when I walked home, I avoided going the shortest distance because there were no street lights along that route. Rather, I went the long way around, several blocks out of the way, where the street lights were because of a very large black bear that managed somehow to get behind me. Not only did that imagined bear dictate the way I returned home, but he also dictated how fast I got there—running! One particular night I remember feeling his hot breath on the back of my neck. At that time I felt certain that all that would be left of me the next morning was a pair of shoes on the sidewalk where I had been devoured.

'All this had nothing to do with logic. Logically I knew there was no such thing as a bear in the whole area in which I lived. In fact, I never saw one until years later when I first visited a zoo. Yet I was convinced there was a bear lurking in the darkness behind me. At that time I could not have turned around and faced my imaginary bear, even to see that in reality it did not exist. My only solution was to pick up and put down twelve-year-old feet as fast as I could until they were safely tucked in their own bed.

"My fear was real; the bear was not. My thoughts of what would happen were real thoughts, and they were attached to real feelings." We could call the fear felt by this individual a mythical fear. It is somewhat like the fears you may feel when you are about to give up your SDB.

One student in this program stated, "I always procrastinated doing my math assignments every week and therefore did less than my best. I discovered the mythical fear I had was, 'What if I really tried hard and did my best, then found out I was dumb in math after all!' Once I got this out into the open to myself by writing it down, it didn't appear to be such a valid fear after all. So what if I found out I was dumb in math? After all, that's the way I've been acting all these years anyway. But if I did find that out about myself—well—there are other things I'm better at."

This student hit upon a very important concept: Finding out your limitations is not so bad as you might think. Knowing what you can

115

and can't do, what you are and what you are not, is important information to help build what you *can* be and to bring security within. When you try to be something you are not, you are maintaining a self-defeating pattern. However, this awareness of your limitations should not discourage your striving for improving attainable skills. This striving is part of growing and learning. But trying to maintain an erroneous self-image has its prices.

At this point in the program, many have expressed the fear that if they give up the SDB they will become a person who is even more undesirable to themselves. I call this the "all or nothing" feeling. It is sometimes expressed as a fear of slipping to the extreme end of the spectrum, so that the person feels the need to stay on the end where he is, even though it hurts to be there. Hanging on to that end seems to be safer than to risk letting go of the SDB pattern. This, too, is a mythical fear, because it is highly improbable that anyone is going to become opposite in character to what he has been in one step, unless it involves a total conversion from one way of life to another and a better way, such as is seen many times in religious conversion. The truth is that the person will, by giving up the SDB pattern, open to himself the opportunity of experiencing a happy middle ground where he may be more open and genuine with others.

Another fear related to eliminating a SDB has to do with the feeling that the person will need something to take the place of his SDB crutch on which he has leaned for so long. This fear was borne out in the example of a female participant who had experienced periodic severe depressions for over fifteen years. At first, she denied that she had anything to do with becoming depressed. She disowned any responsibility for doing it. As far as she was concerned, it just "happened," and there was nothing to be done except suffer it through. In Step Four she learned about the choices she was making to bring it about. When she realized she was in control of her depression, she first became disgusted with herself for such sneaky behavior, then somewhat fearful as the program progressed that she really could—and should—give up this behavior.

She finally expressed the fear that she would have nothing as effective to take its place. For fifteen years she had manipulated her husband and family members to get what she wanted by becoming depressed, even by threatening suicide. Depression was a somewhat effective way of communicating, though it was also inappropriate and extremely dangerous. After the program she learned to communicate openly and to meet reality as her best and most integrated

116

self. She learned not to allow external situations to depress her. She learned that her real self was enough. She was not created with the crutch; being without it would take some adjusting, but she did it. Nothing more than her best self was needed to cope with life in controllable moments of time.

What Benefits Can I Gain by Giving Up My SDB?

Considering and writing down the positive experiences you may gain by giving up your SDB is of great help.

A participant at a state prison, who was working on stuttering, had for twenty-five years let others do his talking for him whenever he had to use the telephone. He had the fear that if he tried to talk on the telephone, he would not be understood because the other party could not see him. He feared being ridiculed.

In his daily work on the prison grounds, he had to use the telephone in order to be admitted back through a large metal gate into the inner compound where he lived. When he counted the hours of waiting in the cold or in the hot sun for someone else to happen along who could give the request that the gate be opened, he determined to take control over that fear and use the phone himself.

The next time he completed his work and had to reenter the compound, he picked up the phone and made his request. He was successful. The gate opened. He said later that he had begun thinking how nice it would be just to go up to the phone by the gate and call in to ask for it to be opened, then go on through as everyone else did—to shower, eat, and watch a favorite T.V. program— rather than stand out there waiting and cursing himself for hours. Needless to say, he became a much happier man. (Chamberlain, 1976:58-59.)

To eliminate SDB patterns, this fear concept needs to be first understood, then applied. Continue to identify the fears you use to block off the non-SDB road, and as these are brought out into awareness, make choices not to use them. Or, if you project fears down the non-SDB road, check them out to prove to yourself that they are mythical.

Your fears will lessen when you realize that the fears you have of being without the SDB patterns are feelings you have lived with for some time; you have been using behaviors that served to avoid meeting the fears. For instance, if you look at the outcome of your defeating behavior patterns, you see inadequacy, spoiled relationships, unhappiness, loneliness, rigidity, frigidity, irresponsibility, vulnerability, and hurt. In reality, the fears you have of letting go your

SDB patterns become true as you continue to practice these SDBs—but *not* when you give them up. In most cases the *opposite* of what you fear will happen.

Past participants have reported life-giving results as they eliminated SDB patterns and opened up to their own interests, talents, choices, ideas, needs, feelings, and limitations. In a similar way, opening up to other people's opinions, thoughts, and ways of perceiving is helpful, as is opening up to nature, history, futuristic forecasts, a different generation than one's own, and the spiritual universe in the midst of our world. (Cudney, 1975.) Remember, you were created to live successfully *without* your self-defeating behavior.

After you have listed your fears regarding giving up your SDB, look at them carefully and try to see them in the brighter light of your present maturity. Try to view those fears as mythical or imaginary, as irrational ideas put into your memory by some earlier life experiences—ideas that need not be maintained any longer. When you have done this, list on Form B those positive or beneficial things you look forward to in your life without the SDB to encumber you or stop you. The major barrier between your present state and those beneficial things you desire on the non-SDB route is a mythical fear that has thwarted your good intentions and helped keep you on the SDB route. When you have completed Step Six, you are ready to face that barrier. You will do that in Step Seven.

STEP SIX SUMMARY FORM A: FEARS I FACE TO GIVE UP MY SDB   DATE_____

List below what you fear when you consider letting go your SDB. (See examples in the Step Six readings.) Items in the two categories may be interchangeable.

What might you find out about yourself?	*What might happen to you?*

118

_____   _____
_____   _____
_____   _____
_____   _____
_____   _____
_____   _____
_____   _____
_____   _____
_____   _____
_____   _____
_____   _____
_____   _____
_____   _____
_____   _____
_____   _____
_____   _____
_____   _____
_____   _____

STEP SIX SUMMARY FORM B: BENEFITS I WILL GAIN BY GIVING UP MY SDB   DATE_____

List below the benefits you look forward to after you have done away with your SDB pattern.

_____
_____
_____
_____
_____
_____
_____
_____
_____
_____
_____

_____
_____
_____
_____
_____
_____
_____
_____
_____
_____
_____
_____
_____
_____
_____
_____
_____
_____

Critique for Step Six

Review your forms A and B for Step Six. Notice that the fears you have written there on Form A may seem a bit irrational now that you have them out where you can see them more objectively. You may wish to write in the margin next to those fears something like the following words: "These are mental fears I kept going when I was traveling on my *SDB* route. They are mythical fears and are not found on the non-SDB route."
Below are some examples to help you:

Step Six, Form A **(SDB:*Overweight*)**

Things I Fear   My Critique

I am afraid I will decide to blow it before
I get time to adjust to my new self-concept.

If I lose my SDB and thus my barrier of
fat, I will no longer have my excuse for
being unliked or lonely.

I will have to face the idea that if I am

120

not accepted it will be my own fault, not my
body's.

I am also afraid that I've let myself be
bottled up for so long that at the least sign
of affection I'll lose control and do
something I'll regret or that will embarrass
me.

I fear finishing this program and slipping
back into a series of relapses, to be worse
off than I was before.

I fear giving up this familiar SDB because
I will pick up another one, maybe worse,
that I don't know. (Composite entry.)

DAILY DIARY (SDB: Overweight)

Wednesday

In thinking about the next steps in the
program, I feel as if I'm building up to a
climax, which I hope is not as dramatic as
my imagination wants me to think. I still
decide to put flashes of eating through my
mind although I haven't allowed myself to
carry out the necessary outer moves to
execute the SDB. Yet the non-SDB
behavior feels un-me still. But I am trying.
My fears of giving it up are starting to rear
their ugly heads. Dealing with them in this
step has helped me to see them more
clearly as only fears I carry around in my
own head. They are not out there in reality.

Thursday

In so many ways I have paid painful and
costly prices for my SDB behavior. I have
felt like a bystander watching others enjoy
life. So I turned to reading books, telling

These are all mythical fears I have kept going to scare me into staying on my SDB route. They are not real and are only kept going because I continue to travel on that route. They will not occur along the non-SDB route.

I can see how irrational these fears really are. None of them could happen unless I go to great effort to *make* them happen. But since I am in control of what I do, that can't happen.

My Critique

I am trying hard to keep my SDB intact by frightening myself with all the imagined negative possibilities without it.

But I am in charge of my outer movements, so that even if I do *think* these things, I can still be in charge of what I *do* about such thoughts. I am tying myself into reality better, too!

I am seeing myself more clearly than before and gaining new insights into my behavior.

myself that I was vicariously experiencing
events of classic depth and magnitude. Ha!
Vicarious living is dead!

I also used to convince myself that by
suffering I could become "Sally Sensitive"
empathetically understanding the despair of
others. But now I realize that before I can
help anyone, I must first pull myself out of
the mire of my own SDBs; otherwise I am
one drowning person trying to save another
drowning person—the blind leading the
blind. It doesn't work! (Printed by
permission.)

I am learning what it takes
to really help myself first.

Hang in there!

References:

Chamberlain, Jonathan M.
>1976 Eliminating a Self-Defeating Behavior. Handbook for Education 514Rx-1, a Brigham Young University Home Study course: How To Eliminate a Self-Defeating Behavior, Fourth edition. Brigham Young University Printing Services, Provo, Utah.

Cudney, Milton R.
>1975 Eliminating Self-Defeating Behaviors. Kalamazoo, Michigan: Life Giving Enterprises.

Hill, Napoleon
>1967 Think and Grow Rich. New York: Hawthorne Books.

STEP SEVEN:
FACING MY FEARS
AND DISCOVERING
MY INNER SELF

You have come a long way. Freedom is in sight. You should proceed with this step only after satisfactorily completing Step Six. The step you are now beginning will help you experience the exhilarating strength and freedom that come from destroying your fears and negative feelings, enabling you to face yourself squarely and discover who you really are without your SDB.

You may find it most helpful to complete Step Seven in the presence of a professional helper, a close friend, or a loved one who is willing to read aloud to you the instructions for the "guided imagery" session. Even though someone may aid you in completing this step, your SDB can remain confidential if you wish. One of the reasons for having assistance is that you can close your eyes and imagine each point as it is described to you. Although this step is more difficult to do alone—since you must open your eyes to read the instructions—you can do it by following the directions carefully.

YOUR OBJECTIVES FOR STEP SEVEN

You will be able to:

1. Face at deeper levels a mental barrier keeping you from traveling the self-enhancing, non-SDB route.
2. Identify the origin of your self-defeating behavior and see that you no longer need it.
3. Rid yourself of your self-defeating self-image.
4. Visualize yourself coping in life without the self-defeating behavior.

HOW TO PROCEED

1. For those of you using this book to participate in a group workshop, your leader will take you through a simple process that will help you meet your barrier to being your best self. For individuals, the instructions are printed here. You will be guided in a step-by-step manner through a mythical or imaginary barrier. In this "guided imagery" session, you will be asked to close your eyes and imagine certain ideas and experiences.
2. Read "Facing Those Fears," following.
3. Arrange to be in a quiet place, either in company with a friend, a loved one, or a helping professional, or alone where you can listen, think, and react for about twenty-five minutes.
4. Listen carefully and concentrate deeply on the ideas expressed; then respond to the instructions to the best of your ability. If you are doing this alone, you may respond to each point along the way.
5. After listening and responding mentally or verbally to all the instructions, write your experiences and learnings from this guided imagery session on the Step Seven summary forms.
6. Continue to write in your daily diary as before.
7. After you have completed the above activities, you may go on to read Step Eight.

Facing Those Fears

In this step you will be taken through a mythical barrier that has blocked your non-SDB route for you. It is necessary for you to face this barrier and go through it, around it, or over it to become yourself without the SDB. Listening to the instructions (with your eyes closed) will assist in helping you to visualize a barrier and to work through it by using a method called "guided imagery." It is not hypnosis. The instructions are very simple. You will be asked to close your eyes so that you can concentrate and introspect. You will be asked to imagine a physical barrier of some kind (something in your way that keeps you from going forward). When you have this barrier pictured, you will be instructed further what to do. It is normal for you to feel a little apprehension at this point in the program, but don't let that stop you.

Afterward, you will see that your fears about going through this experience were also mythical. It can be a most meaningful experience, enabling you to go on without the SDB and its attached prices. Try not to break your mood of concentration. Relax and follow the instructions carefully.

You should not listen to these instructions until you have completed the first six steps of this program; it may be to your disadvantage if you do.

You are to be respected and admired for the efforts you are making to eliminate a self-defeating behavior. What you have done thus far has taken a great deal of courage and stick-to-it-iveness. I sincerely hope my personal and sometimes very frank comments in this book have not only been of help to you during your efforts to go through this program now but that they will be of help for many years to come. When you have completed this program, you may gain additional insights if you refer to these steps and your diary often as you apply the ideas to other SDBs.

Having successfully or partially internalized and applied the basic principles and information from the previous steps, you are now ready to face your mythical fears and to look at yourself at a deeper level. You are ready, even if somewhat apprehensive, to let go of your SDB. The following points will help you face your mythical fears and move beyond them to become the healthy, happy, confident, and creative person you really are. Because I am not there in person to help you with this important experience, you will have to help yourself with a few mechanical things. After you read each point, or after it is described to you, pause. During this pause, try to experience what you have been asked. When you have achieved each point, continue to the next one. Further instructions will be given you along the way to make it as easy as possible for you. You are ready now for point one.

Guided Imagery

If you are having someone help you with this guided imagery session, have that person read the following instructions to you, pausing at the appropriate times indicated in parentheses. If you are alone, close your eyes as much as you can to visualize what you are asked.

The following should be read aloud:
1. Close your eyes and keep them closed until I instruct you to open them. If you wear contact lenses that annoy you when your eyes are closed for twenty to thirty minutes, you may wish to remove them. However, you may open your eyes at any point along the way if you feel the need to do so. Normally, the experiences you are about to have are more effective if your eyes are closed.

Now, with your eyes closed, I want you to imagine a physical barrier of some kind—something in your way, something that keeps you from going forward. Relax. Let your mind bring into it whatever it will. Try to visualize this barrier. It need not have any connection at this point with the SDB you have been working on. Make the barrier as physical and as real as you can. Give it size, shape, color, and texture. Note its thickness or how tall it is or how wide. Note where you are in relation to it. Imagine this barrier clearly before going on to the next point.

If for some reason you are unable to picture an image of some kind but instead are thinking about a concept, or words, note what they are. But still continue to try to visualize a barrier. If you should visualize several, settle on only one. Everyone experiences his or her unique barrier at this time. (Pause.) If, after a minute or so, you see nothing but darkness and are unable to imagine a physical barrier, use the darkness as the barrier and picture yourself within it. Take your time. Let your mind come up with whatever it will. Pause now until you have been able to imagine some kind of a barrier, even if only darkness. When you have pictured a barrier, signal by raising your hand slightly, then proceed to the next point. (Reader, pause in silence until the subject's hand is raised.)

2. Now that you have pictured a barrier, focus on that barrier. You must find a way through, around, over, or under the obstacle blocking your way. If your barrier is darkness, you must find a way out of it into the light. You can create anything you need to help you get out of or to the other side of the barrier. You *must* get to the other side, even if you have to struggle to force your way. You must see yourself reaching the other side. When you have done this and can see and feel that you have made it to the other side of the barrier, signal by raising your hand, and we will continue to the next point. (Reader, pause in silence until this has been done. Allow whatever time it takes, then say, "Very good.")

3. Now that you are on the other side of the barrier, note any differences compared to where you were before. Look around and observe whatever you can. (Reader, pause in silence about five seconds.)

4. Now turn and face the barrier and thoroughly, totally and *completely* destroy it so that nothing is left of it and so that it cannot be there ever again. You can do this in any way that you must. Totally do away with it so that nothing remains of it and so that it can never be in your way again. When you have done this, raise your hand. (Reader, pause in silence until this is done, but be cautious. If, for some reason after trying for several minutes—four to five—to do away with the barrier, this person is unable to indicate so, go on to

the next step, saying: "That's all right you may want to come back to that later if you can't do away with it right now." Then skip point 5, and go on to point 6 below).

5. Now that you have done away with the barrier, notice how it feels to be free from it. Also notice that you are now free to go forward and backward without the barrier in the way. Notice anything else that you can do *now* that you could not do before with the barrier in the way. (Reader, pause in silence about five seconds.)

6. Now stop imagining this scene regarding the barrier. Go back in time to recall, perhaps when you were younger, much younger, when you first began to feel the need to do the self-defeating behavior you have been working to eliminate. Recall an experience or perhaps several experiences you had then that are in some way related to the beginning of your SDB. It will be easy to recall these earlier life circumstances. When you have recalled something that seems close to the origin of your SDB, raise your hand. (Reader, pause in silence, allowing plenty of time, but if the person has not raised his hand after three or four minutes, say, "Perhaps you could recall the first time you realized you *had* this self-defeating behavior." Pause until the hand is raised.)

7. Good. Now, still focusing on that earlier experience, recall how you felt at *that* time; note how old you were, what was taking place in your life, and who might have been involved. (Short pause.) As you look back, note how you made some kind of an erroneous or untrue conclusion about yourself or about the way you must behave from then on. Or realize an erroneous self-image you have been maintaining since then by doing your self-defeating behavior. See as clearly as you can as you look back on that earlier experience from your more mature mind that in some way you may have been acting logically and intelligently for you at that particular age and in that situation. See now more clearly that it was an erroneous learning you have tried to maintain by doing your SDB since then, and put those earlier experiences in their proper perspective in your life.

When you are able to recognize an erroneous conclusion or learning about yourself that you have been trying to keep going by doing your SDB, raise your hand. (Reader, pause in silence until the hand is raised. Do not be alarmed if the person sheds some tears at this time. Keep on to the conclusion of point 13. For those who were unable to destroy the barrier in point 4, say: "Now go back to the barrier you had imagined before and note whether there is anything different about it. Perhaps you could destroy or change it in some way now." Wait for the subject's hand to rise.

8. Recognize now that you have worked through your mythical fear, and you have destroyed the barrier it represented. You have seen what may be the real cause of your SDB, or something close to that original cause, and the circumstances surrounding its origin in your life. If your SDB was caused by someone, perhaps you can see now that that person was acting out of his or her own SDBs and was not made fully aware of the reaction created in you. See and *feel* that you no longer have a *need* to do your SDB. Do not concern yourself at this moment about what will happen to you *without* it. That will be taken care of in a few minutes. Just let yourself feel deeply, "I no longer need to do my SDB." It has hurt you long enough. You have paid many high prices for doing it. You were all right without it before you began to do it, and you will be all right without it now. When you can feel deeply and perhaps see clearly that you no longer need to do it, raise your hand. (Reader, pause in silence until the hand is raised.)

9. You may be experiencing relief to realize deeply that you no longer need to retain a behavior that has hurt you so much. Now see yourself totally free from your SDB. Imagine yourself without it. To help you do this, imagine you are split into two people. One is the person you *were* with your SDB, and the other is the person you *are* without it. Separate these two images of you so that you can see them as clearly as possible. Notice how different they are, how they contrast to each other, what they both might look like, what they might be doing, and how they both might feel. When you can picture these two images of you, raise your hand. (Reader, pause in silence until the hand is raised.)

10. Very good. Now with these two images in mind, note that they are incompatible; they do not belong together. One of them *must* go. Now totally, thoroughly, and completely do away with the self-defeating image of you. Do this in any way you must, but do a thorough job of it so that person cannot come back again and so that all that is left is you *without* your self-defeating behavior. (Slight pause.) If you don't like violence, you may wish to see that self-defeating image of you growing smaller and smaller and smaller until it ceases to exist and is totally gone. (Pause.) When you have done away with the self-defeating image of you, raise your hand. (Reader, pause until the hand is raised. This may take a few minutes. If the person, after three or four minutes, has been unable to complete this step, offer words of encouragement such as, "You can do it," or "You are the creator of that image, so you can do anything with it you wish," or "Your life will be so happy without that self-defeating image of you." But do not say much more than this. Then wait for the hand to raise.)

11. Excellent! Now that you have rid yourself of your self-defeating image, focus on the person you are without it, free from your SDB. Hold that image of you in your mind and fix it in the front of your forehead as if you were planting that best image of you there, where you can look up with your mind's eye from time to time in the future and see yourself at your best. This is the person you were created to be. That is more nearly the real *you*. When you have that image of you fixed in your mind, raise your hand. (Reader, pause in silence and wait for the hand to raise.)

12. Very good; now with that image of you at your best, free from the SDB, firmly planted in your mind, go one step farther and integrate that best-self image of you into your physical body, so that you feel this integration, or merging, taking place. Let that image of you come inside your physical body and be at home there so that you can feel and know "This is who I am, *now!*" This is the you that you were created to be. When you feel this merging has taken place within you, raise your hand. (Reader, pause in silence until the hand raises.)

13. And now, one thing more. As the integrated, best-self you are, imagine going down your normal road of life, meeting those old situations that used to bring about the SDB. But now, as the integrated person you are, your best self, free from your SDB, see yourself passing by those tempting or trying situations and feeling good about doing so. When you have imagined at least one such incident in which you stayed on the non-SDB route, you may open your eyes. (For the reader-helper, this is as far as you need to go. Thank you for your help.)

Congratulations! You have made it through the barrier, destroyed it, discovered the origin of your SDB or something close to it, put it into perspective in your life, felt that you no longer need to do it, seen yourself free from it and going along in life without it. You have done away with a negative image of you. How does it feel?

Being Realistic about Change

Don't be surprised if everything looks just the same as before. You may feel at this point that you had expected a miracle to happen, and it didn't. Rather than expect a 180-degree change in direction after this moment, you might look for a one- or a two-degree change. You are now on the non-SDB route and at the *beginning* of a long and happier journey through life. In a thousand-mile journey by air in a straight line, a one-degree change in direction can put the airplane several hundred miles from the original destination. So you see that a one- or two-degree change in direction is an important, though small, change at first. You will probably feel some differences in a few days if you have not felt them now. Furthermore, you may note at points along your new route that you are behaving differently from the old SDB pattern, and you haven't even a desire or a need to do it any longer.

Remember, this experience was not magic. You will still have to control your choices and techniques in order to remain on the non-SDB route. And because you have felt some changes occurring within you, you have not necessarily changed the environment around you, which may still serve to trigger off the old pattern of behavior. Those situations will yet arise in which you will be tempted to relapse into the SDB again. But the need to do it has lessened, if not disappeared. And, as many have experienced, "It takes all the fun out of a relapse."

Keep that best self-image of you fresh in your mind until you get used to being that person. Let it grow and develop, because that is the person you really are. Let yourself feel the freedom from the old SDB in your daily life. Choosing to nurture and maintain that image of you will be more exciting than you can imagine.

Some few participants in point 9 of this session created two images of themselves, neither of which was acceptable, making difficult the choice of destroying one of them. In such cases I have instructed them to simply imagine a third, more acceptable image, one with whom the person could identify and make a part of the self-image described in 11 and 12. This technique has worked satisfactorily for those few people.

For example, one female client imagined two opposite-looking people—one very thin and the other very fat. Her SDB was compulsive eating. She did not want either of them to be her best self; so she was able to create a third image that was somewhere between the other two extremes. It was interesting that she imagined the thin person too thin, sickly, and unhappy and thus undesirable. This was a way of hanging onto her old, overweight self-image and was related to her mythical fear of becoming too thin and unattractive and unhealthy. It was part of the need for doing the SDB.

Continue to write in your diary and to critique it as you have been instructed. Many find that writing down a problem helps to solve it; it can then be seen, described more accurately, and examined more objectively than when it is carried around in the mind.

You may feel that letting go of your SDB has made you into someone new and different. Some people report an empty feeling as though something inside them were really gone. If you do experience this feeling, it may last a few days, during which time you should experiment with your integrated best-self. Try some new interpersonal skills or improve upon some old ones that are self-enhancing. Remember you *can* trust yourself to know what to do and to be the creator and the doer of your non-SDB responses. You can experiment with your new self-image by doing many things to enrich your life. *Make* them be self-enhancing.

You will discover that control over your choices will be much easier to achieve when you operate from a new frame of self-reference. Things may look a little different—even fresh and new—from the non-SDB route on which you are now traveling. Taking this route one step at a time and one day at a time is the way to reap the beneficial rewards at the end as well as all along the journey of life. If you do this, there is nothing in this world that can stop you from your realistic goals.

STEP SEVEN SUMMARY FORM: MY SDB WAS
_____ DATE _____

Check each appropriate response.
I did this alone_____, with a friend or relative _____, with a professional_____, psychologist_____, psychiatrist_____, social worker_____, other_____.

Complete the responses that apply to your experiences in the guided imagery session.

1. I_____ _____ able to picture something as a
    was   was not
    barrier.

2. I_____ _____ able to get through, around, under, or over
    was   was not
    the barrier.

3. The barrier I imagined was (describe the barrier in detail):
_____
_____
_____
_____

4. I did not imagine a barrier, but had thoughts of (describe thoughts):

_____

_____

_____

5. After getting to the other side of the barrier, I _____ _____ able in some way to destroy it.
    was   was not

6. If you were able to destroy it, describe what you did to destroy it:

_____

_____

_____

_____

7. When I went through or destroyed the barrier I _____ _____ notice anything different about the
    did   did not
imaginary scene I pictured. State here noticed differences, if any:

_____

_____

_____

_____

8. I _____ _____ able to recall one or more earlier life
    was   was not
experiences that seem to have something to do with the beginnings of my SDB.

9. The incident/incidents I recalled was/were ... (briefly describe what happened then). I was about age _____.

_____

_____

_____

_____

_____

_____

10. I _____ _____ able to recognize an erroneous learning
     was   was not
about myself resulting from that earlier experience in my life.

11. If you were able to do this, state what the erroneous learning was: (For example, "I decided, why try, someone else [mother] would do my task for me if I put it off long enough; I learned I didn't need to assume responsibility, and that became my SDB.")

_____

_____

_____

_____

12. I _____ _____ able to visualize my integrated self free
     was   was not
from my SDB.

13. If you were able to visualize yourself in this way, describe briefly what you were like:

_____

_____

_____

_____

14. I feel that this experience in "guided imagery" _____ _____ a positive experience for me.
     was   was not

15. If the guided imagery session was beneficial, state the best you can why it was.

_____

_____

_____

_____

16. If it was not, state why you feel it was not.

_____

_____

_____

_____

17. The entire program _____ _____ helpful to me.
           was   was not

18. Indicate to what degree you were able to eliminate your self-defeating behavior by circling the appropriate number on this scale:

WOW! I no longer do my SDB 1	Considerable change but not completely 2	Noticeable change 3
Very little change (some, but not much) 4	I do my SDB just the same as before the program (no change) 5	

19. By circling the appropriate letter on this scale, indicate to what extent you followed the instructions in each step of the program and tried to apply it to your own life.

A   I did every step as directed and tried my best to integrate each one into my life.

B   I did most of the steps and tried fairly well to integrate them into my life.

C   I did some of the steps and tried to integrate some of the ieas into my life.

D   I read through the steps but did not try to apply them to my-self.

E   I neither read nor applied the steps.

20. Write below any additional thoughts, feelings, or remembered experiences related to your experiences in the guided imagery session that you may want to retain for future reference and possible discussion with some trusted person for deeper self-understandings.

_____

_____

_____

_____

_____

_____

_____

_____

_____

_____

_____

_____

_____

_____

(Adapted from Chamberlain, 1976).

Critique for Step Seven

After you have completed the survey regarding the guided imagery session, there is really nothing to critique except your diary. Below is a sample from a diary typical of many responses from those who have completed this program through Step Seven.

DAILY DIARY (SDB: Overweight)	My Critique
Friday	
I'm truly convinced that today was a monumental turning point in my life. All the lessons of this program culminated in the guided imagery session, and suddenly all the concepts are internalized. My ever-present rumbling or trembling has dissipated. It's as if the electric current of anxiety always running through me has finally been shut off. I'm not even worried about my SDB anymore.	Congratulations! I did it. · Terrific progress!
Saturday	
It's a lucky thing the diaries are being phased out because mine would get rather redundant; all I can say is that my SDB is really gone and it's a glorious feeling! Best of all there is not even any inclination toward my SDB; so the thought of overeating doesn't hold any tempting power for me. That really attests to the deep-down removal of the cause and not just the symptoms. It seems that I was afraid to succeed, so by developing a self-debilitating SDB I tried to insure my failure. But I'm not afraid anymore.	I may feel an empty feeling for a few days, but it is worth it. Now I can make progress in other areas of my life too.
Sunday	
I think one of the best effects of not being encumbered by my SDB is that I can be less self-absorbed about my	I am maturing out of an old hangup.

135

*inadequacies. Knowing, really knowing, that
I am in total control frees me from fear of
failing. So now I can feel less self-conscious
and enjoy the company of people without
feeling inferior and inhibited.*

Monday

*It is still hard for me to grasp the impact
this program has and will have on my life.
I'll go for hours completely free and happy;
then I'll pause, and it will hit me "It's gone,
really gone!" I fully know it now, and that
realization periodically hits me anew,
accompanied by a thrilling feeling that is
ineffable.*

I am *on* the non-SDB route and I *feel* it.

It feels good to be in control of me.

Tuesday

*It's exciting to get up in the morning now
because I can look forward to a day of self-
mastery. I have already felt the program's
concepts generalizing to other of my less
severe SDBs, such as procrastination.*
(Printed by permission.)

Happiness and joy, here I come!

References:

Chamberlain, Jonathan M.
   1976 Eliminating a Self-Defeating Behavior. Handbook for Education
      514Rx-1, a Brigham Young University Home Study course: How
      to Eliminate a Self-Defeating Behavior, Fourth edition. Brigham
      Young University Printing Services, Provo, Utah.

Sharing Experiences

After experiencing the impact of Step Seven, people who are in my regular ESDB workshops share their experiences. They do this for several reasons: one is that they need to know they are not alone in what they imagined, and that they are not "crazy" because of the unusual things that happened in the guided imagery session. Another is that they may receive additional help in understanding possible relationships between the things they imagined and their real-life struggles. While some barriers are quite obviously related and symbolic of the problem or may represent a hidden aspect of the SDB, not all are related to it.

The majority of people imagine some kind of a wall as the barrier. These walls have been described in a variety of ways, from smooth steel or glass to rough, jagged brick and weeping mortar or stone, to the massive and "eternal" Wall of China; from small two-feet-high walls that can be stepped over or around with ease, to walls that are infinite in height, length, and depth. Some people picture formidable and seemingly impenetrable rivers, castles, cliffs, forests, or mountains, while others imagine food, such as giant ice-cream sandwiches, blocking the freeway for miles, or a giant marshmallow or chocolate-drop cookie. Some see a person as the barrier to their progress. Some see only thick darkness and are able to get out into the light.

Their methods of getting across or out of the barrier are typically climbing ladders or trees that grow conveniently nearby or grasping grappling hooks and ropes slung over the top—even climbing ropes to helicopters that lift them up and over the barrier. Some slug their way through to the other side with their bare fists; others kick the barrier down or blast a hole in it with dynamite. Some use heavy earth-moving equipment to move large sections of it out of the way and to destroy it later in the same way. Many blast the wall to pieces, clean up the rubble neatly, plant grass over the spot where it was, then dance back and forth over that spot to make certain of the complete freedom they feel.

Typically, people see the other side of the barrier as being lighter, more pleasant and inviting. Some see green valleys, grass, and trees with streams of water and flowers. Others see nothing different on the other side.

Breaking through the barrier seems to represent a symbolic breaking out of a long-held habit into a new life. As one person described it, " I have just broken out of my 35-year-old cocoon and can now spread my wings and be what I was created to be." After destroying the imagined barrier, a person has a typical feeling of great accomplishment and success related to the feeling of being in control over his or her life. Breaking through it, then destroying it in some physical way seems to represent the kind of all-out exertion needed to put the SDB in its place once and for all. Even though later a few people revert to a semblance of the old SDB pattern, they still report having known the "taste of victory" and know they can do it again *if they chose to.* For many people the barrier seems to symbolize reducing the SDB to rubble so that it can no longer dictate behavior or hedge up the way to greater happiness.

If you are undergoing therapy with a professional helper, you might gain further insight into your personal problems by discussing with that person the possible meanings of your imagined experiences in the guided imagery session.

You may see yourself in some of the shared experiences following the guided imagery session. Further research is being done on the effects of this session alone without the other steps preceding it. So far indications are that it is a most helpful and simple therapeutic tool.

Molestation

As I write this I am reminded of a nineteen-year-old female college student we will call Sue, who had been severely depressed and suicidal for some time and was receiving therapy from a female colleague of mine. My colleague had participated in the ESDB program prior to this incident and realized the value of it as a therapeutic method. When Sue related to my colleague that she felt a black core of some kind inside her body, my colleague requested that I treat her with the guided imagery technique. I consented on the basis that it would be experimental and that I would not guarantee results in one short visit.

Sue came with her female counselor to my office. She was reluctant to trust me while she closed her eyes. I spent much of the forty-five-minute session building enough trust for her to begin the guided imagery. When she closed her eyes, I instructed her to describe the black core inside her. She described it vividly as about two feet long, a black pear shape with a gooey texture. I instructed her to imagine cutting herself open and taking it out; she did. Then I asked her to destroy it. She attempted to destroy it by cutting it into small pieces, but each piece grew back. It was seemingly impossible to destroy. She struggled for a few minutes. Then I instructed her to stop imagining it but to leave it there; we would come back to it later. I instructed her to recall when she first felt it there. She thought a few moments, then began to cry and would not tell exactly what had happened; it was too humiliating to her. In some ways, she was unable to tell it. She did say it was something that happened when she was about three, and it had to do with her father. From her implications about this childhood experience, I surmised that it was related to if not actually sexual molestation by her father. She confirmed my supposition by a nod of the head. As I questioned her, she was able to see the erroneous conclusion she had come to about her part in the experience. She could see that it was not her doing, that her father had a problem for which she was not to blame.

We then switched the scene back to the black blob. I asked how it looked. She replied that it had changed in texture, that it was now very hard, like black glass. She took a hammer and smashed it into thousands of pieces and saw a whirlwind suck up the dust and pieces until it was totally gone. She described her body as well again where the black core had been for so long. Opening her eyes about twenty minutes after she had closed them, she was a different girl, relaxed and no longer fearful of me or the situation. She sat quietly in deep thought for a few moments with tears running down her cheeks, unable to speak. (Printed by permission.)

My colleague reported later that she had improved so much by the next visit they decided to terminate therapy. My colleague followed up with occasional calls for several months and reported that the subject continued to improve and had no more depressed bouts.

The part of the guided imagery session dealing with a specific look into the past is usually most revealing to the individual about

himself or herself, who recalls long-forgotten incidents that had triggered off an erroneous self-image. Now the individual is able to see
these incidents in their true perspective because of a greater maturing that provides a more realistic view of what happened. It also becomes apparent to the individual that he or she had learned an erroneous self-image and had maintained it by using self-defeating
behaviors. Many times, a young child will, in a moment of great
stress, anxiety, anger, or fear, come to a damaging conclusion about
himself, coloring later perceptions of himself and others.

Compulsive Handwashing

On one occasion while I was working with inmates at a state prison, a middle-aged Mexican-American whom I shall call Pete ap-
proached me with the problem of compulsive handwashing. This
problem had plagued him most of his life. During regular group
therapy sessions he had had to leave the room to go to the bathroom to wash his hands. At first I assumed that he had a kidney or
bladder problem, since he would excuse himself two or three times
in the weekly hour-and-a-half sessions we held. Then he told me he
left to wash his hands each time and that he could not keep from
washing them whenever he had an opportunity.

What I did to try to help Pete I had never done before. In that
moment I thought it would be worth a try. Before this incident I had
used the guided imagery method only at the conclusion of the regular ESDB program. But at this time I felt that Pete could be freed
of his problem if I used it without the other steps. To test his ability
to see images, I told him to sit on the chair, close his eyes, and
imagine whatever he wished for a few moments. Pete described a
peaceful scene in the mountains where he was fishing in a mountain
stream, with grass and meadows, birds, flowers, and trees surrounding him. He especially expressed feeling the freedom the surroundings represented. I asked him to stop imagining that scene and to
go back in time to the moment he had first begun to feel the need
to wash his hands so often. He immediately recalled a traumatic
scene that had occurred when he was about six. He was to take
some food to his older brother, who was isolated in another part of
the house because he was ill. Pete saw his brother, covered with
bleeding sores and scabs and scratching himself in pain, and he
dropped the food and ran and hid. He concluded at that time that if
he could keep his hands clean, he would never get what his brother
had. It worked. He never did get it. Thus the handwashing behavior
had been continually reinforced. Now Pete almost shouted, "I don't

need to do that any more!" I then had him imagine himself going along in life without this behavior pattern, living normally. He could imagine that very well; so I instructed him to open his eyes.

In the conversation that followed, I asked him in the group if that problem had had anything to do with his divorce. He then clapped his hand to his forehead and said, "That's it! I could never figure out what was wrong. She was the most beautiful girl, and I loved her a great deal, but I could not stand to eat her tortillas or anything she fixed with her hands. I always felt there was something very wrong in our home. I would not allow her to invite any of our relatives to visit us because of this feeling. I could hardly stand to have her touch my body. Now I know that it was the eczema she had between her fingers on one hand that bothered me so much." We discussed the subconscious connection he had apparently made between the fears attached to that earlier childhood experience and the flaky skin on his wife's hand.

He confessed that he had been so fearful of her touching him that on the occasions when she indicated she wanted to have sexual relations with him, he lied to her and schemed ways to avoid that physical contact. On one such occasion when he had nearly run out of excuses, he felt the only way out was to bandage up his genitals and tell his wife that he had had an accident at work. He bandaged himself accordingly. Of course, she wanted to look, and she saw the bandage. Immediately she called the doctor, realizing he had not yet seen the doctor. So he found himself in an interesting predicament—on his way to see the doctor with his insistent wife. He knew that when the doctor looked he would find nothing wrong; so he managed to excuse himself when they got there, and in the bathroom he scratched himself so that when the doctor examined him he would find a real wound. The doctor did find the bad scratch, gave Pete some ointment, rebandaged the wound, and sent him home. Pete said he had thought that scratch would do him in, it hurt so much.

On my next visit a week later, Pete and his friends greeted me with smiles. One of them could not wait to tell me what had happened since I had left the week before. He began by telling me that in the fifteen years he had known Pete, the day after I left was the first time he had seen him without his fingernail clippers digging and clipping at his fingers to get all the possible dirt from around and under his fingernails. Pete confessed that in the fifteen years he had spent in prison he had not been able to eat the noon meal because he always spent that time in the bathroom getting his hands per-

141

fectly clean to eat with. By the time he was satisfied they were clean, lunch time was over. Now he was working in the automotive center, in minimum security. The day after my last visit when the noon whistle blew, he had had grease all over his hands. He took an old rag, wiped them off, and went to eat. He showed me his hands, front and back, almost every week for the following fifteen months, and usually he would say, "Look, Doc! Dirty hands." He was cured.

As a result of this experience the word got around in the prison. The guards told me I had the first voluntary waiting list for group therapy they had ever seen. Many of the participants were Mexican-Americans. (Printed by permission.)

Homosexuality

A twenty-four-year-old male in one of my workshops who was trying to overcome homosexual behavior went through guided imagery with me in my private office. When he closed his eyes to imagine a barrier, he became quite upset. I had him describe what he was experiencing as he went along. He described a large mound of live nude male bodies. As he attempted to approach this barrier that he created, he became frightened. He said he was fearful of becoming one of the mound and of losing his identity as a person. He attempted in several ways to break through the mound. For some reason he felt that he had to go through it rather than around it. Finally in great fear and with tears he said he could not do it. He had seemingly imagined a barrier impossible for him to surmount.

I asked him to stop imagining the barrier and to go back in time to recall when he had first begun this self-defeating behavior. He recalled that his father had died when he was about twelve. His memory of him was as an emotionally cold, nonaccepting father, who never showed any physical affection toward him. Since early childhood he had craved the warmth of his father's approval, his arm around him in love. But he never received these things from him. Thus, he recalled that when he was about fifteen an older man showered him with attention, praise, and physical affection—something he had always missed and needed. The man, however, engaged him in homosexual behavior.

The conclusion to which my client had come at that age was "How can this be wrong, when it fills such a need in me to be loved by a man?" He could now see that this was an erroneous conclusion and that through a series of circumstances he had been led, at first innocently, to that way of thinking. He had succumbed, then, to the temptations that led into a "gay" life.

I asked him to return, in his imagination, to the barrier he had described. When he did, he explained that something had changed. There was now a large opening through the mound of bodies, like a hallway cut through to the other side. As he began to walk through it, it suddenly collapsed around him, and he tearfully described the horror and panic he felt. Then, still with eyes closed, he struggled physically to work his way through the mass of imagined bodies until he became physically exhausted. He had by this time struggled for over 1½ hours. Time did not permit us to continue, so we decided to stop the session and have him return the next day.

The second day he recalled the same barrier and again struggled physically with arms and hands grasping the air to free himself. He finally described taking a large, sharp knife and swinging it violently from left to right, cutting his way through the imagined bodies. As he described this image, his arms swung back and forth, his face grimacing and teeth clenching as he hacked his way through. But as he was almost through, he physically gave out and began to cry, sobbing that he could not make it; he had run out of energy. But in one last effort he began to make swimming motions with his arms, declaring he could see a round opening in the distance; and if he could just get to that opening, he would be through it. I told him that if he could put one hand through the opening, I would help him by pulling him out. After a time he said, "OK, my hand is out." I took his hand, and he seemed to leap forward, still in a sitting position on the chair. "I'm out!" he cried. I'm out, but my foot is stuck!" He worked to get his foot free, then sighed in great relief and relaxed for a moment as he said almost in a whisper, "I have just been born!"

I instructed him to destroy the barrier. To do this, he saw it getting smaller and smaller as he saw himself flying upwards away from it. He described himself in the clouds above the earth. Looking around, he saw his deceased father with outstretched arms, beckoning him to come to him. He wept profusely at this·point as he described going into his father's arms and being enveloped in love by him.

He enjoyed this touching scene for some minutes. Then he described seeing a person of great light whom he recognized as the Savior. His arms were also outstretched and beckoning him to come. As he did, he said tearfully: "The Savior also loves me and forgives me." Then he wept silently for some minutes. I asked him

143

to return to the earth again. He said he did not want to, that it was so very good to stay there near the Savior. But finally he said, "I guess I have to go," and described himself back on the earth where he could see many such mounds as the first one. But now he had no fears, no homosexual desires. He stated that he had no reason for them any more and that the idea was repugnant to him now.

He began to shake his left hand as if trying to shake something off. I asked what he was doing. "I am turning white throughout my whole body, and the only place still dark is my left hand." I told him it would become white when I touched his hand. I did, and he said: "Now it's all white and clean and pure. I am all clean again." I instructed him to open his eyes. Two hours had passed. He had to go to a lab class at the university. Since he looked exhausted, I asked if he did not want to stop and rest before going. He declined and left.

The next day he related that others who knew him—his landlord and his roommate—saw in him noticeable changes and commented on those changes. They both asked if he was on some kind of new drug. He replied that his old behavior was so disgusting to him now that he could not imagine having done it. The semester ended about three weeks after this incident, and during that time I saw him twice a week. He reported having new interest in his schooling and in the opposite sex, and he had not visited a "gay" bar once during that time, which was a record for him. He also reported that he had not been involved in any sexual behaviors. This was a significant change.

I did not see him again after that, nor have I heard from him since. I am hoping that he has closed the door on that past and has gone on to be himself at his best, learning long-forgotten and new social skills in the process. During the process of the ESDB Program, he had written such things in his diary as: "Help! This is scaring me to death!" "What will I do without my SDB? The gay life is all I know." This fear was great within him.

But he had discovered that, contrary to the popular teachings about homosexuality, he was perpetuating it by his own choices. He was not created to be homosexual. (Printed by permission.)

Fear of Suffocation—Claustrophobia

A group of American Indian clients all of whom were adult social case workers on a reservation went through the ESDB Program with me as their leader. A middle-aged female would not come completely into the room where we were conducting the workshop. Her

144

SDB was a fear of suffocating in a room with people in it. This fear had been with her as long as she could remember. When she closed her eyes in the guided imagery session, her barrier was a dense reddish fog on the other side of which was a large turtle. She struggled to get through the fog, saying: "I have got to get through to the turtle before it disappears." When she finally broke through, the turtle had disappeared. She was puzzled about this and asked what it meant. I asked the same question of her. She said: "My fear is gone! But why a turtle?" We both puzzled over that one and came to a dead end. When I asked her to recall when this SDB first came into her life, she described the feeling of being crowded in the dark and could not breathe. She felt this experience so strongly that she became frightened to recall it. For one hour she tried to recall what had happened earlier in her life to cause this reaction. (At this time in my experiences with this method, I was taking from one to two hours per person to help him or her through the guided imagery experience because I had them describe in detail each imagined scene or action while I wrote it down. I have since learned that large groups of people can have the same or similar experiences in much less time.) The hour with this client was up. I asked her to return in the afternoon for a group sharing session in which each participant could share what had occurred in the private guided imagery session with me. She went away puzzled. Later in the day, she returned with a wide smile on her face. She said that she had discovered finally what it was all about. When she was about two years old, her uncle used to tend her and her baby brother on the reservation, and "when he grew tired of watching us, he would either hang us on a nail on the wall, or put us under a wooden box." Her face suddenly lighted up. "That's the turtle!" She described remembering that it was dark and crowded and there was no one to hear their cries under that box. In the circle a few minutes later all the participants, having gone through their own experiences, were eager to relate what had happened to them. This client sat in the circle and wept silently. When her turn came, she told the others that this was the first time in her life she had been able to do this. When she was asked, "Do what?" she said: "Sit in a room like this, with people in it. All my life I have had a fear of smothering in a room with people in it, and at school, church, or anywhere people met, I always had to sit in the doorway or outside where I could get out quickly and get some air. Now it's gone."

We corresponded for six months following this incident, and she reported, "It is still gone, thank you!" (Printed by permission.)

Childhood Illness

In this group was a handsome male Indian, about twenty-seven, who was somewhat reluctantly working on feeling unlovable as his SDB. His described experience in the guided imagery session was as follows: He imagined a cabin in the mountains and saw himself approaching it down a trail that went around it. On closer examination, he discovered there were no doors or windows in the cabin. Suddenly he was sucked into the cabin through the chimney and could not get out. After a search he found a brace and bit and drilled a hole in the wall. As he made this hole, a cone-shaped, stainless steel object came inside toward him. There was a very small hole in the point, so he made himself small enough to climb into that hole and escape. When he was through that, he found another barrier—a cement wall. He pounded his way through it with a large sledgehammer; then he was kept from going forward by a barbed wire fence. He cut the strands of wire and went through the fence. Suddenly he was confronted by a sheet of white fabric, like gauze or mosquito netting. This frightened him, and he began to cry, and said he could not go any further. He did not want to know what was on the other side, nor could he break through it in any way.

We shifted the scene to have him recall when he had first encountered such feelings or such an object. He described seeing himself at about age two in a hospital crib with bars all around and springs over the top so he could not get out, and the whole thing was covered with mosquito netting. Through this he could see his parents and a nurse, and they were talking about him and to him: "But they didn't pick me up and hug me or cuddle me as they used to. Something is wrong with me." Then he paused and amid more tears said: "I had tuberculosis! I was in the hospital for nine months. No wonder my parents didn't want to kiss me. They didn't want to get it." He realized that he was lovable after all and that he had come to an erroneous conclusion about himself because of that earlier experience.

As you can imagine, with each new group going through this experience, many experiences could be written, some of them tragic in nature such as the following one that occurred while I was working with inmates at a state prison.

Criminal Behavior

A forty-one-year-old inmate whom we will call Jim had gone through several marriages, had written bad checks, was alcoholic,

146

and had been in constant trouble with the law since his youth. In the guided imagery session he discovered that he had not killed his little brother, as he had believed since he was seven. He saw clearly for the first time that the death of his six-year-old brother was an accident. His parents had told him to watch out for and be responsible for his little brother. The day before school started, they were both excited, especially since the younger one was to start school for the first time. Jim ran across the street that day and did not know that his brother was following him. His brother ran into the path of a car and was killed. Jim concluded erroneously that he was to blame and felt that his parents blamed him also, although they never discussed with him his feelings or what had happened. Their silence was taken by this seven-year-old mind as a clear accusation of his guilt. He took on a "bad boy" image and perceived the reactions of others as threatening and negative from that time on. He seemed to be looking for ways to punish himself for his "guilt." When he "saw" the accident in this moment of relaxed recall with more mature eyes, he wept and repeated over and over: "I didn't kill my brother. I didn't kill my brother . . . ." His countenance changed as well as his behavior. He later met a fine woman who came to the prison in a family home evening program there. They fell in love, and when he was released a few months later, they were married. In the last report about him, four years later, he was working as a counselor with alcoholics in a live-in center made from an old church building, and he was using the ESDB method as part of the treatment program. (Printed by permission.)

Impression from Infancy

I have become more and more fascinated at the ability of the human mind to recall incidents from very early life. The earliest impression recalled by one participant in this program were strong impressions of rejection at six weeks. In a recent ESDB workshop conducted by one of my graduate students, a mother and her daughter were participants. The daughter was about nineteen. Her SDB was centered around compulsive eating with feelings of rejection and lack of self-worth. In part of the guided imagery session she saw something that brought deep feelings and tears. At first she was reluctant to describe what she had recalled because it was "too far out" and too disconnected with any conscious experience in her awareness to make any sense to her. She was, however, encouraged to tell what she had seen, and she finally did. She told of seeing herself as a small baby in a bassinet or crib and seeing her father

147

coming toward her and rejecting her; then he turned away and picked up and loved her older sister who was standing nearby. She said, "That is ridiculous, because I have never seen my father." At this point her mother, who was present in the group, began to cry. She said: "Oh, yes, you have. When you were six weeks old, your father came to visit us, and he came into the room. You were lying in a bassinet; he took one look at you and said, 'What an ugly baby. What are you going to do with that?' then turned and picked up your four-year-old sister and hugged and kissed her." (Printed by permission.)

It seems that impressions are left with certain individuals in moments like these that are not erased. They are difficult for the individual to understand at those early ages and can influence behavior throughout one's life. This and other similar cases have led me to believe that infants and young children learn much more than we adults think they do and that their minds are like computers absorbing impressions thousands of bits per minute, which are recorded there and stored. We who are parents must be careful not to create SDBs in our innocent children in a thoughtless moment.

Biting Fingernails

A brilliant, single, twenty-seven-year-old female professional enrolled in my ESDB workshop with the purpose of working on her fingernail-biting behavior. When she closed her eyes in the guided imagery session, she saw the barrier as a rather clear plastic sheet that separated her from her mother. She tried to get through to her mother but could not, and no matter what she did to the plastic sheet it would grow back again. She considered her mother to be very beautiful and herself to be ugly. She had always felt that her mother did not accept her because of this. After trying unsuccessfully for some time to get through that barrier, she was asked to go back to a time when she first began her SDB. She then recalled an incident that occurred when she was three years old. She was sitting on the curb beside her three-year-old friend in front of the house where she lived. He was reading to her from a comic book. She thought: "I am smarter than he is, but I don't know how to read." So she ran into the house and begged her mother to teach her how to read. Her mother put her off, telling her that she would learn soon enough when she was old enough to go to school. At that age, this little girl had concluded erroneously, "I know why she will not teach me how to read; it's because I'm ugly." This erroneous self-image was upheld in the years to follow in her own behaviors;

biting her fingernails was one supporting behavior that represented a very ugly way to keep her hands. After discovering what she felt was the origin of this behavior and its related manifestations, she was asked to go back to the plastic barrier and see if anything had happened to it. She was amazed to find that it was melting away and that she could reach through and be in the full presence of her beautiful mother. Her mother loved and accepted her after all. This was a joyous feeling to her.

She returned to her parents' home the next month. For the first time in about eight years she spent the summer with her mother. When she returned in the fall to resume her employment, she looked more feminine, was well dressed, used makeup, and was decidedly a more attractive female. She soon met a graduate student; they fell in love and married a few months before leaving the area, and during that time she returned to another ESDB workshop to work through another SDB. This one had to do with feeling competitive with men, and in particular with her husband. She described it as a feeling that she always had to prove she was smarter than men. This was disruptive to a good relationship in their marriage. No doubt she had a superior intelligence, but she did not want to discourage her spouse's efforts to be successful. The second time through the guided imagery session she saw the barrier as a brick wall that completely encircled her. It was a prison from which there was no escape. She finally managed to push it over, but there was still no way out of either the top or the bottom of this cylinder. She finally had to call for help from her husband, who she imagined was walking around on the outside. He came to her rescue and knocked a hole in the top.

Her feelings of gratitude for his help, the realization that she did not know all the answers, and the knowledge that he had his place in her life were revelations to her. She also realized that she did not have to be constantly proving herself and her intellectual abilities; she could live happily without having to prove anything. When she recalled the origin of this SDB, it was the same incident that had occurred when she was three. However, in that incident she also concluded that she had to prove to boys that she was better than they were at many different pursuits. This led her to a tomboy pattern of behavior as well as the SDB she was trying this time to eliminate.

The conclusion of this session was that she felt much more relaxed around men, especially her husband. She could genuinely support him in his successes and trials. In the weeks that followed this session, she reported several times that it had made a great difference in their relationship. She has been back a few times to show off proudly two lovely children. (Printed by permission.)

Felker (1974) said, "It is often said that the past cannot be changed. This is true, but the inference that there is nothing one can do about the past is incorrect. One cannot change the past, but one can change the meaning attached to past experiences. It is not necessary to continue looking at things as one did as a child. One of the steps individuals need to take in the process of improving the self-concept is to reinterpret the past so that the meaning of past experiences is changed, especially if the experiences were negative." (Pp. 28-29.) This statement is proven many times over in the ESDB guided imagery session.

As individuals are able, often for the first time as an adult, to see more clearly the earlier life experiences that in some way were related to the beginnings of an erroneous self-image, they are then able to gain new insights as to their meaning in their lives. New meanings can attach to old experiences, and in so doing they can release the psychic energy that was needed to maintain the old and hurting interpretation. As one participant put it: "Suddenly, I am grown up."

Childhood Accident

Another participant in this program had not completely eliminated her barrier the first time. In the next session, sensing that she had not resolved the problem within herself, I asked her to reimagine the wall she had pictured in the beginning. She had imagined climbing the wall on a ladder, then dropping down slowly on the other side with a rope. However, she had not let go of the rope because there was a dark hole beneath her, and she could not see the bottom. I asked her to let the rope extend downward so that she could explore that dark hole as an experiment and see what was down there, knowing it would now be safe to explore it. She described herself going down into the hole, still hanging onto the rope. As she did, she expressed seeing first gray smoke, then flames, coming up below her. She began to shake physically and to cry, saying it was burning her. Then she imagined water was covering her body, and she was playing in the water. She remembered that at about the age of one, she had been playing around flames, and her dress had caught fire. She was burned over most of her body. She recalled her mother rushing to get water on her and taking her to the doctor.

150

This incident was a significant beginning to her self-defeating behavior, which had to do with distrusting happiness and distrusting God. She said her erroneous conclusions at that early age must have been: "You can't trust happiness, because it will turn into pain suddenly, like having the rug pulled out from under you." At this point, as a mother of three children and contemplating a divorce, she felt she could see more clearly what she must do, that she was truly in charge of her own happiness and that it could be trusted. She indicated that it seemed as if she had been in a state of shock ever since that burn, and she had just now come out of that traumatic experience after approximately 28 years. (Printed by permission.)

Those who picture their barrier as a person, such as a father, a mother, or a spouse, usually find it more difficult to "destroy." This may be because of the guilt feelings about harming another person even in imagination. Many have worked around this by changing some disliked or frightening aspect of the imagined person in order to render that individual more acceptable in some significant way. Others have been able to change something in themselves to make the two of them more compatible. Some have seen the threatening person disarmed of excessive power. One person saw her human barrier nude, and that rendered him humorous and therefore less formidable as an authority figure in her life.

Feeling Worthless

One elderly lady saw her deceased mother as the barrier who was keeping her from approaching an important box. The box turned out to be her father's coffin; her mother was keeping her from looking into it to see her father's body at his funeral service. This had occurred when she was four. The scene was made vividly personal in her mind by the fact that she had to come to the funeral in a borrowed dress that did not fit and was not to her liking. The feeling of being worthless began in her life at that time. She concluded from that experience that she would never wear a homemade dress again because it symbolized the feeling of poverty this incident initiated in her. After harboring these feelings for over fifty years, she was able to rid herself of them and became interested in learning how to sew her own clothes. After that she vowed not to wear "store-bought" clothes again. (Printed by permission.)

Fear of the Dark

Another woman, whose life's story would make an epoch film, could not see or imagine anything but darkness when she closed her eyes—a darkness frightening to her. Upon exploring it, she could see a slit of light at the lower edge of what looked like a door, and she recalled more than one frightening experience from her early childhood. One was being locked in a closet by some of her uncles and left in a state of semiconsciousness for most of a day. She wrote: "My mother died in El Paso, Texas, during the flu epidemic. My baby brother was buried with her. My dad tried having his first wife help him care for us children. I heard her say she would take the boys, but she wanted none of me. I had my mother's name, and I was nine years old; so sometimes Dad would let me stay with my grandmother. One day my uncles were doing some repairs and sent me after some nails without heads. I went. The men at the hardware store laughed at me, so I ran back. My uncle was very angry, so he locked me in the closet and went after his own nails. They forgot about me. I can remember how afraid I was."

Her earliest recalled experience also had to do with the dark. It occurred in Mexico in about 1912, when Pancho Villa was ravaging the colonies of Americans in that territory. "Dad had saved the life of Pancho Villa; so on this night (I was about 2½) Pancho Villa told Dad his men were going to be in Guadalupe, where we lived. At about midnight or after, Dad gathered up his two polygamous families and carried my half-sister over to my mother's root cellar with her two brothers and her mother. My mother was six months pregnant with my brother .... This root cellar was about 8 by 12 feet, containing boxes and nail barrels and foodstuff. So there were my three brothers, my mother, and myself, besides those he brought, making a total of three adults and six kids besides me. There were no lights; shooting was going on outside, and hatred was inside between the two families. Is it any wonder I have fears in the dark?" With rifle shots punctuating the total darkness, with spiders, cobwebs, and the musty odor of this old cellar, despair and utter helplessness gripped her. She feared they would all be killed.

In spite of these and many other negative experiences, she had dedicated her life to serving others and to rearing a large family. After working through these erroneous self-learnings, this woman, now in her late sixties, developed a greater eagerness for life and a desire to learn what she could from it. She recently returned from a six-months educational and genealogical tour of England and Europe. She had a minor relapse while she was there: "Once on my six-month's study abroad, the lights were turned off. I had to get out of there; I felt as if I were smothering. I was embarrassed; what would everyone think? But I am triumphing over some of my fears. It is going to take time...." (Printed by permission.)

Psychosis

Many students and professional colleagues have asked if this method will work for the psychotic patient. My learning tells me it likely will not because the individual who is at that state of emotional disturbance is too threatened by the idea of assuming that much responsibility for self-behavior. However, I had one experience with a young woman in her thirties whose husband had heard of my workshops through a friend who had gone through the workshop. She and her husband arranged to spend their vacation where they could both be involved on a private basis in the ESDB program with me. Prior to their visit, her psychiatrist sent me a large file of information regarding the chronic history of severe emotional disturbance in this woman. She had been in and out of the state mental hospital several times in the years prior to her visit with me. She had experienced severe depressions and had attempted suicide. She was labeled "schizophrenic" with little possibility of a cure. However, she and her husband and I were willing to try this as an experiment to see what could be done.

Upon arriving, the woman let me know immediately that nothing would help her. She informed me that she had already gone through more intensive therapy than I could imagine and that nothing I could offer in the way of therapy could possibly help her. She set forth in earnest to defeat the program from the beginning. However, I did not allow myself to believe that it would not help her. The fact that she was in my office every other day for ten days told me she did have hope, even though she would not outwardly admit it, nor would she do any of the steps in the usual way. She continually reminded me that the ESDB program was ridiculous and would not work; nothing would. She was beyond help. All she wanted to do was curl up in her bed and remain there. Her husband helped by bringing her to my office every other day for a two-hour session. He, too, worked on an SDB. We finally finished the seven steps, with much arguing over trivial points and with many attempts on her part to avoid going forward.

The guided imagery session occurred the evening before they were to return home to a neighboring state. In this session she imagined the barrier as a hole 160 feet deep. She was in a box at the bottom of the hole. She could see the opening at the top, but she would not attempt to come out of the hole. She finally imagined a small rope coming down. As she took hold of the rope, it fell into pieces in her hand—too flimsy to hold her. Then she imagined a large rope coming down—a rope approximately the size used to tie steamships to the dock. This rope was too large for her to grasp, so she remained in the hole. We struggled for approximately two hours to get her out of the hole; during this struggle she said, "If I get out of this hole, I'll get better, and my husband will not pay attention to me any more." She was obviously fearful of getting out. Her insightful statement seemed to be at the heart of the problem. Her husband had been very gentle and solicitous with her, and in some ways he had assumed responsibility for her behavior. This pattern seemed to create a dependency that may have been detrimental to her. Not knowing what else to do, he had catered to her illness and had perpetuated some of the symptoms in her behavior by rewarding them with increased attention. She took advantage of his gentle nature to her own detriment—the development of her fear that she could not hold him in any other way.

Our time ran out, and I felt obligated to bring her to the usual point of closure of this guided imagery session—the end of the total program. She was still in the "hole," so we arranged to have them both return to my office at 5:00 a.m. the next morning. They had to leave by 7:00 a.m. to drive more than 800 miles to their home.

In the 5:00 a.m. session she imagined herself in a pipe 160 feet deep with no way out. I asked her to imagine that I was going to pour sand down the pipe on top of her. If she wanted to get out, she could move slightly; the sand would trickle past her body, and she could stand on it and push herself up. However, for the next hour and forty-five minutes, she sat absolutely motionless. As I poured sand slowly on top of her, I warned her that she would smother in that hole. But she would not move, either mentally or physically. I filled the pipe with sand, all 160 feet of it, and planted grass over the top so that it could not be found. We left the person that apparently represented her self-defeating image smothered and dead in the pipe.

At that time it was not my practice to have participants do away with their self-defeating images of themselves. She taught me something of value here, as I shall reveal later. The two hours were up. She left my office in what I felt was an unresolved condition.

I was greatly concerned and apprehensive over the outcome of this unusual experience. However, I felt certain that with the insights she had gained in this experience she could not go back to her old behavior pattern. I instructed her husband to call me as soon as they arrived at home to tell me what had happened. He failed to do so. I waited one month after their departure, then finally called him to determine what had happened after they left my office. He said

154

he had forgotten to call, that things were going very well. She had been able to get up in the mornings and get the children ready for school and get him off to work. She had become active again in social and religious activities and had told her psychiatrist "where to go." He said: "Something must have worked. She has been a very different woman ever since."

About three months after this phone call, the friend who had referred her to me called. He said that she was a very different person, that it had made a noticeable change in her behavior, and she was much happier. Three years later, while I was on a speaking tour in her state, she and her husband met me again and told me that experience had been the turning point toward good mental health for her. They were both all smiles. (Printed by permission.)

In my experience with the ESDB theory, I have found it to be rather self-selecting. Those who are unable to go through the steps because of emotional stress are probably not ready to assume that much responsibility for their own lives. Those individuals should receive therapy through other methods. They may eventually arrive at the point where the ESDB program would have an effect in their lives. Further study and research needs to be done on this point. To my knowledge this method has not been applied in psychiatric wards and hospitals where individuals have more serious emotional problems. It seems best suited for those who are fairly normal and able to read, introspect, and write.

Some of the comments that have come back from this experience are quoted here. From one participant:

March 3
"The guided imagery session filled me with strange sensations after we had finished. I didn't know what to think. But as the hours went by, it really helped me to see myself in relation to my self-defeating behavior, and to never want to resort to it again. I felt sick just thinking about my SDB and its harmful effects in my life. I seemed to be totally cleansed and refreshed in a way similar to repentance. I am a totally new person who doesn't even know himself and needs to explore within himself. It seems as if a great weight has been lifted from me, and I don't even know what to do with the new sense of freedom."

March 4
"Today I didn't know myself. I had no thouhts at all about my SDB. I used neither of my labels 'I am inferior,' nor 'I am equal'; nor did I pre-experience any situation. I didn't even think of my bar-

rier or about myself as I saw myself without my SDB. I simply felt great about myself and toward others. All day it seemed as though I didn't control what happened; it just occurred. I can't put this experience into words because I don't think I fully understand what is going on yet. I simply feel totally different and want the feelings to continue on and on." This was from a college student who had overcome feelings of inferiority. (Printed by permission.)

The following quotation is from a graduate student working on severe pessimism:

"I'm really feeling a new kind of freedom for the first time in my life. Actually it's more like a new responsibility, since now that I know the real reason for my SDB, I am totally and consciously making a choice to do or not to do it. It really is a great feeling. From now on, every time I begin to make a situation negative, I see that scene from my earlier life that initiated my SDB, and I think twice before carrying through with it."

The following day, he wrote:

"I'm finding the way I relate to people to be very different from what it has been. Suddenly, I'm talking to them as individuals, not as reflections of my mother, whom I must struggle with for power. I can't believe the freedom and happiness I'm feeling. My wife and I had a short conversation, then analyzed how I am relating to her differently in a much less negative, selfish, controlling manner. Now if I can relate to my mother in a genuine manner without these old feelings welling up, I'm home free." This student reported verbally to me some weeks later that he had had an opportunity to test his new self-image on his mother and found it to be just as effective. He did not slip back into the old pattern of being defensive and feeling overpowered by her. (Printed by permission.)

The following are some quotations from some of my home-study participants whom I have never met. They are from various parts of the United States: "I have been helped from the very first lesson. I feel this program should be given to everyone. The realization that I do decide ultimately what I do and am in control of myself has given me great strength when I am confronted with the urge to do my SDB. Often I remark to myself 'I choose not to do that' and *I don't!*'

Another former participant wrote:

"I marvel at how each step reveals some new self-awareness to me and that with this specialized awareness I gain a greater area in which to make conscious choices. I gained some *freedom*. This is real!" Three months later this participant wrote: "I also feel more at

156

peace with my feelings, more accepting of myself, less self-conscious about how I look. I have more self-confidence, worry less about others' opinions of me."

Another wrote: "Once I accepted responsibility for my actions, I eliminated the guilt feelings I get when someone has to do my job for me. Also, learning that my self-defeating behavior is an action and not part of my personality and that I can change my actions without changing me was most helpful."

One man said, "The mere act of writing in the diary served two basic purposes for me. (1) It permitted me to help myself by making a statement, examining the statement, and evaluating my own behavior; and (2) I was able with increasing forthrightness to communicate with my wife without fear of her reaction."

Still another wrote:

"I felt really blessed taking this course. I have been filled with energy; I feel I can eliminate my other self-defeating behaviors, and I am anxious to begin on another one. In the past month, I have conquered another SDB of laziness. I am now running 3½ miles per day and have reached my ideal weight. *LIFE IS EXCITING!*" (Anonymous.)

And another:

"This workshop helped me because I could concentrate directly on exactly what was happening concerning my self-defeating behavior. It wasn't just 'happening'; I was making it happen, and I could change that. I saw exactly how to catch it, stop it, and change routes." (Anonymous.)

Another said, "This workshop was very helpful to me. I feel as though I will never need to do my SDB again. The insight I have gained into my personal behavior is valuable. I wouldn't trade what I have learned from this course for anything!" (Anonymous.)

The following notes from a first grade teacher, her husband, and students are self-explanatory. (Included by permission.)

THANK YOU FOR A <u>HAPPIER</u> SCHOOL TEACHER!

Eric SusanLyn Kim
Stacey Jenny Cindy
Russell Danny Quinn David
Jonathan Dean Darren Rich
Gene Ben <u>   </u>
Howard Ty Richard
Sheri Michelle. Jackie
Laura

Clare   mon. May. 26ᵀᴴ
sd6. temper
You say the purpose of this course is to help others
come closer to experiencing true joy in living.
Please accept my sincere appreciation for
the greater joy I've found —

                    Clare

I would like to thank you for the
help you have given to my wife! She is
now able to go what seems like forever
without getting mad at me, even though
I may need, or deserve it!

                    thank you
                    Lynn

References:

Felker, Donald W.
    1975 Building Positive Self-Concepts. Minneapolis, Minnesota: Burgess
        Publishing Company.

How to Prevent Self-Defeating Behaviors in Self and Children

This chapter is important because teachers, parents, and children help create self-defeating behaviors in themselves and others. Learning how self-defeating behaviors are developed could help us prevent their development. Now that we have seen how to eliminate self-defeating behaviors, it would be a loss if we did not learn how to prevent them. If I were to summarize this chapter in the fewest of words, I would simply write: How to prevent SDBs? If you are a parent, listen actively and effectively to your children. If you are a teacher, listen actively and effectively to your students. If you are a child, communicate openly and honestly with the adults around you. Honest and open communication is the key to preventing self-defeating behaviors from developing and being maintained in our lives.

This kind of communication includes not only that which should exist between individuals for understanding each other but also positive communication with ourselves about ourselves. This internal communication has been called "self-talk" (Nance, note 1); "self-referent talk" (Felker, 1975); and "evaluating thoughts" (Maultsby, 1975).

What we tell ourselves is most important. These self-referent words and thoughts direct our feelings and perceptions about ourselves. They color the way we receive and interpret new information in ongoing moments of our lives.

Parents and teachers can serve as models for using positive self-referent language in the presence of children. This not only helps children think in more positive and constructive ways about themselves but also helps those who do the modeling.

When we recognize we are in charge of the thoughts we think and realize these thoughts are largely responsible for resulting feelings and consequences, we can choose more wisely to experience enhancing rather than defeating feelings by choosing positive rather than negative thoughts and the self-talk that goes with them from which the feelings and acts stem. Thoughts, like seeds, can bring forth only their own kind. This is a law of nature.

The question always seems to arise: "I am not perfect; neither are my children's teachers and playmates nor their brothers or sisters. How, then, can I prevent my children from acquiring self-defeating behaviors?" It seems an impossible task to prevent these disruptive behavior patterns from beginning in an individual's life because we do not know what seemingly minor incidents will create an erroneous impression in the mind of a child or an adult. Fortunately, we can do something to prevent self-defeating behaviors from occurring. Most of these self-defeating behaviors were created through erroneous impressions about statements that were made or in stressful incidents that occurred early in life. These negative or misunderstood experiences triggered erroneous conclusions about self and in the process created an erroneous self-image. In most cases this erroneous self-description could have been corrected much earlier in life had each individual engaged in more effective internal and interpersonal communication regarding feelings, misunderstandings, and puzzling experiences. Such communication would have resulted in feelings of acceptance and love. Self-defeating behaviors based on faulty perceptions are kept alive and hidden within the individual when either good communication or sufficient love are missing. Communication is usually lacking in moments when parents or other significant persons are busy, angry, or thoughtless. In those stressful moments, people tend to say or do damaging things to children and let the damaging impressions stand unchallenged and unchanged in the child's mind. These negative concepts need to be talked out so that the child does not hold them as negative possessions that hinder individuality and limit or cripple potential. Impressions stored in the mind determine how the mind interprets new information from new experiences. Dr. Penfield (1975), a noted brain surgeon, discovered years ago that the human brain stores away all experiences and impressions, and, under the right conditions, is capable of recalling and reliving any or all of them. Moody (1975) found specific common experiences in near-death incidents of individuals that indicate the mind can recall long-hidden and forgotten acts.

Possibilities for misunderstandings and erroneous ideas of self are always present. No amount of effort by a parent or guardian can control all the experiences a child may have away from home, with playmates at school, or even at the grocery store. Even if it were possible, such control would be detrimental to the child's growth as a social being. In spite of the best efforts of parents to be open and communicative with their children, negative labels are affixed to them by other children, siblings, or adults who have self-defeating behaviors of their own. These negative labels stick and are difficult to remove until the individual gains sufficient and mature wisdom to see that the label does not accurately describe his or her true self. It is unfortunate that so many people go throughout their lives maintaining an erroneous self-image, literally making the negative labels come true. On the other hand, some individuals set out on a quest to "prove" to themselves and others that the negative label is not fitting. They do this by determining to be the opposite of the label, a determination that in itself may not be fitting and is an SDB too because it prevents them from being themselves. They feel they must forever guard against fitting into the pattern that is assumed or implied by the negative label. Children can be taught to check out their "self-talk" for its rationality (Maultsby, 1975). They can be taught to take the non-SDB route at every choice. They can be taught a measure of their true greatness.

Those families in which the children are labeled lovingly with endearing names, such as nicknames, are self-enhancing and positive. In these fortunate families, creativity is not stifled, nor is individuality damaged. To some degree, negative labels create suffering in an individual and shortchange his or her potential. They also help to create erroneous self-images in others who associate with him. The true state of Utopia might be achieved when all the people inhabiting a given place have eliminated or prevented the development of any self-defeating behaviors and have come to know themselves and are known by others as they truly are.

A friend of mine has said many times, "If I could part the veil from your mind and let you see who you truly are, you would be utterly amazed at your greatness. You would find that you are a truly great and noble person." Jesus Christ had a greater understanding of who he was than any other being. Because of this, he could refer to himself with firmness as "I AM." (Exodus 3:14; John 8:58.) Even though such a condition may be beyond our capabilities in today's society, striving toward it brings an inner peace and security not felt along the self-defeating route. The fact that individuals can eliminate from their lives one self-defeating behavior after another indicates that it is an inner desire for most human beings. Eliminating self-defeating behavior represents a singular challenge that can be filled with excitement and success all along the way.

When SDBs Started

Over the years as participants have completed this ESDB program, only about 5 percent could *not* recall a specific age or time when they began their SDB. Those who could not felt they had always had it or that it came about so gradually over a period of years that there was no recognizable starting time or incident. These individuals were mature adults and college students in approximately equal numbers. The oldest participant was approximately seventy-five, and the youngest was sixteen. In the home study program the average age was twenty-eight, ranging from eighteen to sixty-nine. (Chamberlain, note 2.) Those older than twenty-three recalled that some of their self-defeating behaviors began after they were married. This often occurred when they had some difficulty in adjusting to their spouses and to the new roles expected of them in marriage.

According to the analysis of accumulated reports from ESDB participants over a five-year period, the largest number of self-defeating behaviors were created in home situations; the school and other environments were next as offenders. In many school-related situations, children learn for the first time that they are wrong or that they are failures. (Glasser, 1969.) The most frequent ages at which participants in ESDB workshops or programs pinpointed the beginnings of their SDBs were five and eleven. However, from birth to age twelve is the most vulnerable period of our lives, for we are so impressionable in those formative years. Yet at all ages incidents may occur that need to be understood better and placed in their proper perspective in our lives.

How SDBs Started

As great a variety of incidents triggered the beginnings of SDBs as there are SDBs. All of them have some common elements. They were initiated in moments of perceived threat, stress, or anxiety, or, as in the case of some recurring sexual behaviors, in a moment of pleasure. But in all cases the individual doer of the SDB learned some erroneous concept about self from those experiences, either at that time or later.

The self-defeating behavior of one lady was fear of men. As a small child she had been sexually molested by her father. Her cur-

164

rent fears were linked with sex, and she had generalized this fear to a fear of all men. Throughout the years she felt there was a serious problem in communicating with her father. For some fifteen years she had had to maintain a guarded stance around him. She wrote, "I forgave him of everything and truly loved him. But the past, hidden deep inside me, was tearing me apart. I didn't know how to keep it from having that effect on me. Even though I was morally chaste, had excellent grades in school, and had a lot going for me, I had a very low self-image. I felt guilty and sinful." This is a typical negative consequence from such an early traumatic experience. In the guided imagery session this lady saw herself in a small bedroom with walls about two stories high and no doors or windows. No matter how she tried to get out, nothing worked. Then she imagined a friend outside who was able to help her. He broke down the walls, but she still wasn't able to get out. She would always get caught in some way. The friend, a boyfriend, looked at her and said that he truly cared for her. At that instant the walls all crumbled down, and he took her away. But she was not yet free. No matter where she went, a small thread held her bound to the barrier. She imagined herself in more pleasant surroundings—in fields, and at church where the atmosphere was pleasant, peaceful, and beautiful, and where she was very happy. When she was instructed to destroy this house with the unusual bedroom in it, she could not do it. Even though she hated the one room, she loved the house. She said the house must be symbolic of both her love for her father and her hatred of the things he did, symbolized by the bedroom. So she replaced that house with a new one with doors and windows, where she could come and go as she wished. However, in the new house one bedroom door got stuck. She saw herself looking at herself as a child. She felt so sorry for that child that she loved her and held her close and told her not to feel bad; it wasn't her fault. Then she confronted the child's father and told him to leave her alone and to never touch her again. She took the child out of the house and felt the need to get rid of her in some way. She found that very hard because, she said, "I love her; I couldn't just make her vanish. So, I took her to heaven and told the people there to make her happy and be good to her. She loved it there. The child's father tried to get her back, but he couldn't. The door to heaven slammed shut, and the bridge from it to earth disappeared."

She declared that this part of the session had helped her the most. "I saw myself as I am now, as a grown girl. I, myself, took my childhood away. I can go home and be around my father without

165

feelings of apprehension or anxiety. I feel I have control over the situation and any that may arise in the future. He can't get to me emotionally the way he used to. I also have a higher self-image and feel better about myself. I have suddenly matured. I still have anxieties about sex and marriage, but they are not as bad. I know now that with a little more work and time, I can do whatever it takes to cope with the sexual aspects of marriage and that my feelings of apprehension around older men will also leave me in time. I can testify personally that it works; this method works miracles. This one session cleared up a lot of fears I have carried for fifteen years. I'm very happy now." (Composite entries by permission.)

The above is one of hundreds of examples of how SDBs get started in a person's life. Most of them are created in moments of innocence on the part of the sufferer or victim, and most of them are created by the SDBs of others.

It is interesting that the same experience undergone by different individuals may produce a different SDB; for example, a negative rejecting comment such as "You can't play with us" by an older sibling could begin a depression SDB, a compulsive eating SDB, or an excessive worry SDB, depending upon how the individual receiver of that message reacted as a way to cope with the negative message and the feelings created by it. The SDB is also partly determined by how individuals differentially perceive the meaning of the incident at the time of its occurrence. But most likely, the SDB is bound up in what the receiver told himself about the incident as a means of justifying or understanding what took place. What we tell ourselves about such experiences is vital.

Erroneous Learnings

A part of learning SDBs are the erroneous conclusions or learnings related to the originating incident. As you recall, in the guided imagery part of Step Seven the person is asked to think back and to recall any experience that seemed to trigger the SDB. Then he is requested to discover some kind of an erroneous idea he learned from that experience so that it may now be put into more accurate perspective in his life. About 75 percent of the participants have been able to identify some kind of erroneous concept as they looked back in time, while 90 percent were able to recall one or more deeply felt incidents that began the SDB.

These erroneous assumptions were deeply impressed in the mind of the individual because of stress, pain, or anxiety and henceforth became the major receptacles through which the individual perceived himself and the world outside himself in future similar situations. To the extent that the conclusion based on the unusual or traumatic incident was damaging to the self as a person of worth and value, the individual developed levels or patterns of behavior to defend against future hurt of a similar kind. As time progressed, these strong sentries of defense against hurt, originally developed as protectors of the royal person within, became prison guards not allowing the real self to emerge.

All the erroneous learnings discovered by participants in the ESDB program would make too long a list; however, a few are shown below under the SDB they helped to maintain:

SDB: Compulsive Eating

Eating rids negative feelings.
I must eat to keep up my strength.
I must eat to keep Father and Mother happy.
Overeating insures good nutrition.
Eating is a way to get even in sex.
Eating substitutes for love, happiness, and sex.
Eating solves problems.
Eating avoids responsibility.
It is bad to waste food.

SDB: Inferiority Feelings

I can never do anything well enough.
Others know more than I do.
Everything I say is dumb.
Quiet girls get more attention.
If you're not perfect, you're a failure.
What others say is more important.
I am worthless.
I am what others say I am.
I'm not as good as _____.
I can't trust my own judgment.
I can't trust anybody.

SDB: Procrastination

There will always be time later.
I don't have to be responsible.
If I put it off long enough, Mother will do it.
Why finish anything? There will be more to do anyway.
I can put off as long as I want and still get by.
It must be done perfectly or not done at all.

SDB: Fears of People
   I'm a klutz.
   Men are to be hated and avoided.
   People think bad things of me.
   For protection, stay away from the opposite sex.

SDB: Sexual Deviancy
   Masculinity depends on size of genitals.
   Girls are only sex objects.
   There is no other way to feel good.
   Having sex solves problems.
   Sex equals friendship.
   I'm not in control of my sex life.
   I'm a nobody, and sex makes me somebody.

SDB: Depression
   My spouse is everything, and I am nothing.
   Act cold and ugly to be left alone.
   No one loves me if I am pleased with myself.
   When I am depressed, others treat me better.
   Everyone is going to hurt me.
   I'm worthless.
   You can depend only on yourself.
   Happiness cannot be trusted.
   I'm worth only what I can do or produce. (Composite lists.)

The above lists are by no means complete. It seems that each individual creates his or her unique reasons for doing what he or she does. But the important thing is that when these erroneous learnings are discovered, any of us can discard them by seeing them as no longer fitting to us or the situation.

How Effective is the ESDB Program?

Although a great deal more study needs to be made regarding the long- and short-range effects of this program in the lives of individuals, some of the results obtained thus far are encouraging. At the conclusion of the program in both the home study and the regular workshops, in a nonempirical study, participants were asked to rate themselves on the degree to which they felt they had succeeded in eliminating the SDB they were trying to eliminate. Table 1 shows the results from 64 home study participants and 229 regular workshop participants, or a total of 293.

Table 1*

Self-rated degree of success in eliminating an
SDB (where all SDBs are combined)

Self- Ratings	Home Study		Regular Workshops		Total	
	No.	%	No.	%	No.	%
1. No More SDB	16	25	48	21	64	22
2. Considerable Change	30	47	115	50	145	49
3. Noticeable Change	12	19	48	21	60	21
4. Very Little Change	1	1.5	12	5	13	4
5. No Change	1	1.5	2	3	3	1
6. No Response to Ratings	4	6	4	2	8	3
TOTAL	64	100	229	100	293	100

*This table includes the seventy-nine compulsive eaters shown in
Table 2.

In this table 25 percent of the home study participants and 21 percent of the regular workshop participants claimed to have eliminated
the SDB. The sixteen home-study participants eliminated the following SDBs: *compulsive eating: 10; inferiority feelings: 1; depression:
1; self-hate: 2; losing temper: 1; biting fingernails: 1.* The forty-eight
regular participants eliminated the following SDBs: *compulsive
eating: 15; inferiority feelings: 12; procrastination: 7; fears: 7; inability
to get along with others: 1; depression: 1; excessive worry: 1; indecision: 2; compulsive thoughts of harming others: 1.*
Because the most frequent SDB chosen for elimination was *compulsive eating* (including *overweight* and *obesity*), a separate table
(Table 2) is included to show the results of the ESDB method as reported by these seventy-nine individuals.

Table 2
Self-rated degree of success in eliminating the *compulsive eating and overweight* SDB

Self-Ratings	Home Study		Regular Workshops		Total	
	No.	%	No.	%	No.	%
1. No More SDB	10	36	15	29	25	32
2. Considerable Change	10	36	24	47	34	43
3. Noticeable Change	4	14	5	10	9	11.2
4. Very Little Change	1	3.5	7	14	8	10
5. No Change	1	3.5	0	0	1	1.3
6. No Response to Ratings	2	7	0	0	2	2.5
TOTAL	28	100	51	100	79	100

Twenty-eight of them were in the home study program, and fifty-one were in regular workshops. Table 2 shows that 36 percent of the home study participants and 29 percent of the regular participants, all working on eliminating compulsive eating, were able to do so. This is a significantly higher ratio of success than that reported by individuals constituting the study of a variety of SDBs (Table 1). Combining the three top ratings: 1) "no more SDB," 2) "considerable change," and 3) "noticeable change" in Table 2, we find that both home study and regular participants did equally well in bringing about changes in compulsive eating. Eighty-six percent in both groups reported changes. In Table 1, 92 percent of the total participants declared similar changes in the three top ratings. In the combined SDB group, only 5 percent declared little or no change; and in the compulsive-eating SDB group, 11 percent reported little or no change. From these results we could conclude that some compulsive-eating participants accounted for the greater number of successes, while other compulsive-eating participants accounted for the fewer number of successes in eliminating this unwanted behavior pattern. Significantly, however, 75 percent rated "considerable change" or better in this SDB category.

Interestingly, the individual in home study who claimed "no change" was working on compulsive eating and reported having lost fifteen pounds during the six weeks it took to complete the home study program. Apparently, this weight loss was not seen by that person as the change hoped for. This phenomenon alerts us to an awareness that "success" is a word of many meanings and is highly subjective relating to change observed in one's own behavior patterns.

Other Studies

A study by Parks (1975) on college students in the ESDB workshops indicated a significant change in locus of control from externality to greater internality. The same result was obtained by Jensen (Note 4) in a pilot study of indigent high school students. Johnson and Chamberlain (1978) found the ESDB workshop made a significant difference in the ability of smokers to stop smoking. The author worked with a female home study student suffering from anorexia nervosa (fear of eating). She weighed eighty-five pounds at the beginning of the program. A significant change occurred in her attitude toward life, food, and herself. She gained fifteen pounds in five weeks. Coombs (Note 6) reported significant positive change in self-concept among groups of junior college students in California. Cudney and others (1976) reported beneficial effects of this method with groups displaying severe emotional problems, such as drug users, alcoholics, neurotics, and prisoners, as well as groups without severe problems, such as career-counseling classes, employment security officers, and large corporations and organizations.

Reference Notes:

1. Nance, Ralph D.
   1974 "My friend 'RIQ' and 'my fun course in RIQ-ology." In Bishop, Donald F. Self-concept change in sixth-grade children completing an unthinking-rethinking program, unpublished doctoral dissertation, Brigham Young University, Provo, Utah.

2. Chamberlain, Jonathan M.
   1977 A workshop that works, even if you are not there, or how to get rid of your SDB by mail. Paper presented to ESDB Update '77 Conference, Grand Rapids, Michigan (May).

3. Jensen, Jack L.
   1977 A study of the effectiveness of group counseling in positively changing self-image and locus of control of economically dis-

advantaged high school youth. Unpublished doctoral dissertation, Brigham Young University, Provo, Utah.

4. Johnson, E. Kim, and Chamberlain, Jonathan M.
   1978 "The treatment of smoking as a self-defeating behavior and prediction of behavior change and maintenance." Journal of Psychology (January).

5. Coombs, David H.
   1974 The elimination of self-defeating behaviors and their relationship to self-concepts. Unpublished doctoral dissertation, Brigham Young University, Provo, Utah.

References:

Cudney, Milton R.
   1976 Implementation and innovation of the elimination of self-defeating behavior theory. Kalamazoo, Michigan: Life Giving Enterprises.

Felker, Donald W.
   1975 Building positive self-concepts. Minneapolis, Minnesota: Burgess Publishing Company.

Glasser, William
   1969 Schools without failure. New York: Harper & Row, Publishers.

Johnson, E. Kim, and Chamberlain, Jonathan M.
   1978 "The treatment of smoking as a self-defeating behavior and prediction of behavior change and maintenance." Journal of Psychology (January).

Maultsby, Maxie C., Jr.
   1975 Help yourself to happiness through rational self-counseling. New York: Institute for Rational Living, Inc.

Moody, Raymond A., Jr.
   1976 Life after Life. New York: Bantam Books, Inc.

Parks, C. R., Becker, M., Chamberlain, J. M., and Crandall, J. M.
   1975 "Eliminating a Self-Defeating Behavior and Change in Locus of Control." Journal of Psychology, 91, (September):115-120.

Penfield, Wilder
   1975 The mystery of the mind. Princeton, New Jersey: Princeton University Press.

Appendix

Examples of Diaries and Critiques

Case A
SDB: Indecision

Case B
SDB: Lack of Feeling Masculine

CASE A

The following diary (with my comments at the right) is a typical example of the struggles many people encounter in giving up an SDB. No names are given to protect the innocent.

DAILY DIARY (SDB: *Indecision*) Female college student, age 19.

September 17, Monday

Today I began to really think about my problem of not being able to make decisions. I feel that in the past year or two I have made some growth but not enough.

In this ESDB program we are told that the defeating behavior continues because we are afraid of something. I decided I must be *afraid of the unknown consequences of my decision,* or afraid of what I would miss if I make one decision over another.

As far as decision-making goes, I think it is my problem. My dad also thinks it's my problem, and he has pointed it out to me. He advises that sometimes it is better to make a decision and make a wrong choice than to sit on the fence so long. I agree, but something—a fear, I guess—holds me from making my decisions.

I have difficulty even with minor decisions like whether to mail a letter or go to the store first. However, I am slowly beginning to make decisions and act on them. Some of my bigger decisions, like school and marriage, are really starting to

Critique

I am getting on the ball by thinking about my SDB.

Good insight! Fear dictates too much of our behavior, and when it does, it is usually self-defeating.

I am owning up to it, and to how I do a fear of deciding (indecision).

I choose to make even minor decisions difficult for me. Do I tell myself, if I can't even handle these minor ones, how in the

hang on me and drag along. They get tiring, and I want to make some definite decisions and quit dragging around undecided choices that weigh me down.

Wednesday, September 19 [In Step One]

How do I make decisions? Well, I was talking to my brother tonight, and I think he hit it right on the head. He and I both can make a decision, but instead of acting on the decision, we sit and wonder whether or not we made the right decision.

My decisions are based on the following:

1. My inability to say no.
2. The mood I am in at the time of decision.
3. Group influence and my opinion of the group.
4. Values, morals, and sense of duty.

I don't think I disown my problem too much. However, I suppose I might blame part of it on my mother, who made too many choices for me when I was young.

Saturday, September 22 [In Step Two]

Last night I didn't write in my journal. I didn't feel that my SDB had been a problem to me during the day, and I didn't have any thoughts on it.

Today, while I was at work, I noticed a sign on the "surprise" column of the candy machine that said "Sold Out." In that column you don't know what you will get when you pull the button.

Anyway, I thought to myself, "I guess other people must use the surprise column besides me." I wondered if other people do it for suspense, or if they, as I do, pull the surprise knob because they can't decide what kind of candy bar they want. By pulling the knob, I don't have to decide.

I have been wondering if decision-making is as much of a problem to me as I sometimes think it is. Maybe I haven't been confronted with so many decisions lately.

It seems as though I make wrong decisions as to when to do homework, for I often find myself at the end of the semester in a bind as I write a term paper or do a long-term project. However, I can't really feel like naming it procrastination. At least, what I mean is that I don't take pleasure

world could I ever handle major ones? I use this to put more fear into all of them. Being weighed down and tired of this pattern are some of the prices I pay for it.

Good observation! We decide to wait.

Do I hang onto this disowning method? I can now choose to be responsible for my own choices.

I decided not to write.

In this way, I do decide to be responsible for the results I get, and to leave it to the unknown. If I can accept the unknown in this way, why can I not accept it by making a purposeful decision and take the unknown consequences of it, too?

I am minimizing the SDB results here so that I can convince myself it is really not even bad enough to work on.

Good point. Knowing what I "should" do and what I decide or choose to do are two different things. I chose to stay on the SDB route by deciding not to study math.

174

over work. I usually always am busy doing something. In fact, I am never bored—but with few exceptions.

I think I have trouble putting my decisions into action. Take today for instance. I'm having a tough time trying to pick up my math book and study for a test. I have made the decision that I should, but I haven't picked it up as yet.

I will pick up my book and study now. I just remembered we will have to define some words, and the professor said they had to be exact. It is still hard to pick up the book and study, but I just committed myself, so I will—I guess out of a sense of duty now.

I make inner choices that are carried out by a series of "outer choices." An inner choice is a commitment to do it.

Sunday, September 23 [In Step Two]

Guess what? I studied my math last night for a good half hour. It has given me enough incentive to really finish studying well tomorrow morning.

I had a great thought today about my decision-making, but right now I can't remember it. Hope it comes back to me. Well, I can't think of it. My roomy is talking to me. I'm going to bed. Good night. It's hard to think when people are talking to you.

A whole half hour? Did I tell myself that was enough? How will I be more motivated in two days to do what I am slightly motivated to do now? Do I tell myself the future moment will be some kind of magical one by then?

Monday, September 24 [In Step Two]

Hi! I remembered my thought. It has to do with decision-making—sort of. I realized more fully yesterday that I am not making any commitments and setting goals enough. This thought was somewhat brought on by the talks at church. Anyway, I seem to be *afraid of commitment*. I have been taught when I commit to something or start something, I should finish it.

Not a bad teaching!, but I have used it to stop me from starting things I could do. Do I have to see the end in sight before starting the journey? This sounds like perfectionism. What would happen if I did not finish something I started?

Monday, September 24 [In Step Three]

I read the comments in the book about my SDB and how it is my problem and that I carry it on by choice. I agree it is my problem, and I don't blame anyone for it now. I do resent the statement that I now carry it by choice. I think I carry it, rather, because I didn't identify the problem for awhile and have not as yet found any suggestions on helping me make decisions.

I guess what I wrote just above sounds like a SDB, and possibly is; but just the same, I do not accept the statement that I carry my SDB by choice. I *want* to change it. Possibly subconsciously I hold onto it, but *maybe I need something to replace my indecision* and fill that gap of

I do not like to appear foolish. It is hard for me to admit that I really do choose to do my SDB. It makes me angry that this program does not tell me exactly what to do about indecision. I want someone else to tell me so that I do not have to rely on my own judgment and work it out for myself. Self-discovery is not handed to me from someone else; it must come from within. It is

175

"losing my blanket" like Linus's blanket in "Peanuts."

Well, I guess I'm looking for a set, straight answer as to how to make decisions. In Education 200 class today, we went through some steps that may help in decision-making:

First, identify the problem.
Second, make value judgment.
Third, weigh consequences.
Fourth, make a plan for new or changed behavior.
Fifth, execute plan.
However, no set rules are going to be handed me. So what must I do? Do I place enough values on this problem to do something about it? I don't feel I do it right now. However, when indecision arises, it bothers me and makes me feel confused and frustrated to the point of feeling that I have a real problem.
In making decisions, I should stop for a minute and think before I speak and commit myself to anything. That would eliminate anxiety caused by [fear of] wrong decisions. I should also stop to consider priorities in my life. Then I can label things to some extent and place first things first. What about the decisions, though, that have no real first priorities? How do I decide those? Good night. I've *decided* to quit writing tonight!

Tuesday, September 25 [In Step Three]
I didn't seem to have any problem with

a disowning statement. I want someone else to be responsible for my progress—also I used the sneaky technique of "impatience" to help keep my SDB going. Also by saying "subconsciously" I am disowning responsibility here too. Who is in charge of my subconscious mind? I am.

Now I am reacting here to the fear I have of what will happen or what I will use to take the place of my SDB. I can choose to develop self-enhancing ways to deal with situations that demand a decision. I can choose to trust myself. I already have in me what it takes to do it! I was created to succeed at living happily.

This is a "set answer," but now I am faced with the decision to apply it or not to my daily living.

I am doubting I have what it takes. I choose to let my SDB really bother me so that I can feel down on myself and use that feeling to prove I am no decision maker.

My indecision pattern is coming out as a way to avoid responsibility for my own behavior. By doing an indecision, I can put off action until others or circumstances take over and decide for me. Thus, I am not responsible. What a cop-out. And how sneaky.

Did I think too much or not at all before I said anything?

176

decision-making today. It was just one of those days that everything I said seemed wrong.

Wednesday, September 26 [Step Four]

Today in workshop a few thoughts went through my mind. One was that by eliminating the behavior of being indecisive, possibly I will need to replace it with decision-making. I also realized that often, instead of making my own decisions, I ask people their opinions. After I get two or three other opinions, I find they either conflict with each other or my opinion; then I stay in a state of confusion instead of making up my own mind.

Brilliant deduction. But I allow it to scare me.

What I was really doing is deciding to avoid responsibility by getting myself confused to keep myself from going in any one direction. Another sneaky technique that works to keep the SDB going! I am learning!

I believe I must be *afraid to some degree of what people might think of me;* so I want to make the same decision as they would make. I think this happens only when I am unfamiliar or unsure about a decision. When I have a definite opinion or have made a decision, I usually haven't much problem in keeping it.

I decide for them what they will think of me; then I react toward them as if they really do think that. I can choose to let them do their own thinking.

The price I must pay for my self-defeating behaviors:

frustration	careless looks
anxiety	too little time
not knowing myself	lateness
tired feeling	restlessness
depression	unhappiness
lack of motivation	lack of confidence
little progress	little enthusiasm
self-consciousness	no zest for life
poor health	no independence
bad attitude	feeling of worthlessness
poor eating	lack of spirituality

(These are some very deep prices to pay for this SDB. I am convinced I *need* to and *must* give it up!)

Thursday, September 27 [In Step Four]

Today I was studying in the library when a problem I have started to nag at me so that I couldn't study. My problem is being afraid to make a decision about marrying a certain fellow. *I simply won't make a decision.* I dropped my homework and sat down to analyze the situation.

I have decided to put off making this decision.

The prices I was paying for not having made the decision were not being able to study, irritable

Good insight! I am learning to think more clearly now.

177

and restless feelings, discouragement, and buying a snack I didn't need, thus wasting money and possibly some time.

I noticed while I was at the vending machine that I hesitated for a few minutes, then made my decision. (Hooray!) I am beginning to think that maybe I should decide what I want to eat *before* I go to the machine, then keep that decision.

Great. Keep it up. Even small victories add up to winning the total war.

Anyway, back to the other undecided choice of whether or not to marry. I have, for the time being, made the choice *no*. However, it is subject to change in time. I think I need to realize that I must forget the choice I'm confronted with and just enjoy the relationship on that basis. If I realize for a while that I don't have to make a decision *now*, maybe I won't have to pay some of the prices for indecision. I'm not trying to avoid the decision. I'm just feeling unready for it yet. I have weighed the consequences in saying "yes" and "no" and I will say neither for the time being. In the meantime, how do I cope with the indecision? Do I need to realize more prices that I must pay before I will decide?

Great insight.

But I am deciding not to decide.

But I have decided to say "no" and that is a decision.

Perhaps I have a fear of marriage or of men? Could this be behind the scenes—pulling my strings?

Monday, October 1 [Step Five]

I have begun to have a lot of thoughts about decision-making. I wish I had written them all down as they came up.

Somewhere in the last three hours I have made a decision about a problem that has been bothering me about marriage. The man I've been dating has helped me a lot. However, I have decided to tell him no about marriage. I still want to be his friend, but the last two hours I have been on cloud nine because I made a decision! I defeated my SDB by making a decision! I feel so good inside.

Great. I knew I could do it.

As I read through Step Four again on internal and external choice, I found in words what my problem is in making decisions. It says that my being without my SDB frightens me; and when I respond with a non-SDB choice, I revert back to making an SDB choice. *That* is exactly what I do. I make a decision; then I hum-haw around trying to decide if it was the right decision. When I make a decision, *I must follow through with the act,* then evaluate to see if it was a good choice. *If it is good, great! If it is bad, well, I'll do better next time.*

I am seeing things more clearly all the time.

About this marriage problem. I decided maybe I'd marry the guy. So I had fun with him and grew in the relationship. As our friendship grew, it was harder for me to see clearly what I myself really wanted. I had done much thinking and praying about it, and still I couldn't seem to reach the answer. Of course, I was looking at it positively, thinking and hoping the answer would be yes. After I would tell myself yes, I would start doubting myself again. It has been said that "when you meet the right one, you'll know." I made the decision to take that statement to heart.

I was writing a letter the other day. As I reread the letter, I noticed that I wrote "I think . . .". That is not a positive statement of a yes or no or "that is the way it is" statement. When I say "I think," what I am really saying is, "I'm not sure it is right, or I don't know for positive." That is indecision. I think (oops, I said it again) just let me rephrase that from "I think" to "my next step will be" to my next step, which will be to say positive statements only.

Way to go! Right on!

Wednesday, October 3 [In Step Five]

As for the big decision I made a few days ago about marriage, I wish I could describe on paper how good I feel inside. Of course, the hurt of memories will be with me for a while, but I discovered that the hurt now is not comparable to the anxiety of indecision before.

I think that way down deep inside me I knew the answer was no; but out of fear of making a decision, I kept myself in a confused state so that I began to think I didn't know the right answer.

The state of keeping myself in confusion is my technique. I am beginning to see the technique used in other ways; I label it *procrastination*. However, I get out of the word procrastination by saying I am too busy. The reason I am busy, though, is so that I have a good excuse to procrastinate. For example, my bank statement: I tried to figure it out and couldn't find my error, so I keep letting it sit. It doesn't bother me enough, I guess. Actually, I'm ignoring the issues to keep myself in a state of confusion.

Being too busy is also a technique.

I don't understand why I would want to hold on to such a security blanket as confusion. Some security! I will be on the look out for my SDB. In the meantime, I will get some sleep. I am defeating my health by staying up late. I must evaluate the SDB that causes my lateness to bed. Could it be indecision?

Catching on very well!

Monday, October 8 [Step Six]

I have been slothful in my writing. I also missed a class last Friday, which I regret. However, I made the decisions and must take the consequences.

I have filled my time with many things the past week and I have decided to not make time to think about decision-making. I am noting, however, that I am beginning to take on responsibility for my actions rather than blame them on someone else.

Excellent!

I have made the decision to stay up late and get up early for the past week or two. This causes me to feel tired, and I find I can easily blame mistakes and inefficiency on tiredness. Instead, I need to realize I myself made the decision to be tired, even though I don't like it.

The price I pay for that decision is general rundown health and disinterest in school and everything else. I need to make a decision. I need to change. I think one of my techniques is not wanting to change even if it is for my own good.

Good insight here. My understanding about self and these SDB's is progressing very well.

Wednesday, October 10 [Step Six]

I was beginning to think I was conquering my problem of indecision until I went to the workshop Step Six on fear. I realize that I really do have a fear of finding out how dumb I am when I make my own decisions. I fear what other people will think of my decision unless I have something definite to back it up with. I'm afraid to discover what I really am for fear I won't like what I find. Thus, I try to avoid finding myself by letting other people make decisions for me.

And by this SDB, I keep me from discovering my true self.

I have a fear of changing when I find out the real me has lots of changing to do. Instead of letting it bother me, I pass it off and tell myself it doesn't really.

Monday, October 15 [Step Seven: I will describe her experiences in the guided imagery session below]

She imagined her barrier to be a huge brick wall. She was very near it. She said, "It is so tall I can't see the top of it and so wide I can't see the ends of it in either direction."

To break through this barrier or to find some way to get through to the other side, she imagined herself walking along one side to the left and said, "I just walked out there and found a door." When she walked through the door, she felt she

180

had just walked out of the town to the outskirts of a small, nonbusy street of the town. This new side of the wall had vines growing on it and shrubs around it.

To destroy the wall completely in some way so that it would never be there again, she said, "I made it disappear." She then could see the rows of shrubs where the wall had been. She said she felt more freedom to pass back and forth.

I instructed her to recall a specific situation wherein she had first felt the need to be indecisive. She replied that when she was younger she used to ask a lot of questions; then she realized she should make decisions on her own without bothering other people so much. In the third grade, she had reading problems and wanted to read a library book, but the teacher had her stay after school in the slowest reading group to work on their workbooks.

"The teacher would give me. the answers because of her impatience at my slowness, and I had mental blocks about knowing what the answers could possibly be. I would wait for her to give me help, and she always came through."

When I asked her, "What did you conclude from these experiences?" she replied, "I concluded that if the teacher had helped me to read a library book rather than the workbooks, I would have relieved myself of the mental block." She further volunteered that she found the seventh grade very difficult and always got "Cs" on her report card. Also, during her seventh and eighth grades, her family had moved to a new school. There something changed, and she got better grades. Before that time, however, her father did half her homework; she depended on him or someone else to do it, not realizing she could have done it by herself. She always feared deciding answers to problems for fear it might be the wrong answer. Her parents assumed more responsibility for her schoolwork and for solutions to problems.

When I asked her to see herself as her best self without the self-defeating behavior, she saw herself with her roommates. She was not asking for their opinions on small things like what color of paper to use on a poster or what she should wear. She said, "I see myself talking to people about things I don't know about. I am listening and I am *learning*. I am not pretending to know, and I am making decisions by myself. It feels pretty good. I can have more sense of direction and more positive feelings, and life is more interesting." She expressed other positive feelings about her future outlook with this different and more positive feeling about herself.

(Printed by permission.)

CASE B

George W. (fictitious name), thirty-three, was a married man with two sons and two daughters. He wrote the following for his ESDB program. I wrote the critiques as the entries were handed in twice a week.

(SDB: *Feeling of male inadequacy and lack of masculinity.*)

Step One Summary: *What I Do and How I Do It.*

1. I compare to my own traits what I consider to be masculine traits in others.
2. I notice the physique, chest hair, and size of genitals of other men and compare my own to them.
3. I search for ways to see how much chest hair other men have.
4. I look through magazines for pictures of shirtless men.
5. I fantasize about changing the amount of hair on my chest.
6. I make myself worry that other men think I am inadequate because of lack of hair on my chest.
7. I make myself lose self-respect because I convince myself it is not normal to have this preoccupation with masculinity traits.

My Critique

I choose to compare with selected others so that I can keep this SDB going, and it works very well! I am selective in what I choose to compare so that of course I can come off feeling bad about myself.

I scheme up ways to keep myself feeling inadequate. I choose to look for these items in magazines to remind myself in as many ways as possible of my inadequate feelings.

I choose to think for others, and of course I can always manage to think they think the worst of me so that I can keep this SDB going. I even can use what I do as proof that I must be bad off, or I would not even do it. This way I can feel inadequate as a person.

Step Two Summary: *How I Disown Responsibility for my SDB.*

1. I blame my inadequate feelings on the fact that I lack hair on my chest. If I had a hairy chest, I would feel adequate.

I choose not to accept my physical body as it has developed, and I blame it for

182

2. I blame my dad for not helping me develop interest and skills in sports.

3. I blame other men for being so smug and satisfied in the shower room about their masculine traits.
4. I can't help it; my mind does this automatically and makes me remain on the lookout for these traits that I feel I lack.

Step Three Summary: *What Prices I Pay for Doing It.*

1. I experience a great unhappiness in myself for being so concerned with this unnatural fear.
2. I have a lack of self-respect.
3. I waste time looking for masculine traits in others.
4. I have guilt feelings over this abnormal worry about traits.
5. I miss many interesting and beautiful sights while I look for chests to observe.
6. I withdraw from conversations with others because of my preoccupation with this SDB.
7. I fear that my children would lose respect for me if they knew.
8. I lose friendships because of the fear people might discover my SDB.
9. I pass over informative articles in magazines because of my looking for pictures to compare myself with.
10. I lose energy because of the nagging guilt that I am not normal.
11. I have depression caused by self-doubts created by my SDB.
12. I feel shame, brought about by my fears that I am not normal.
13. Friendliness toward others is locked within me and cannot come out for fear they will discover my inadequacy.
14. Barriers exist between me and the opposite sex because of this preoccupation with my SDB.

not looking like everybody else's.

I can choose to feel adequate regardless of what my body looks like.

My dad makes me do it now, in these fresh, new moments of living?

They *make me do my SDB? Their bodies make me do it?*

My mind makes me do it, but who is in charge of my mind? I am!

These are just some of the many high prices I have been paying for keeping this SDB going. It is not worth all this.

183

15. I miss out on comradeship with groups of men because of the fear that I am not the same as they are.

DAILY DIARY:

Monday

I worry a great deal about the lack of hair on my chest. The other men in our family have very hairy chests, but I have none. I am continually admiring the hair on other men's chests and am envious of those with this masculine trait.

I choose to worry about this rather than accept what is. Does worry add hair on my chest? No. Poor me, I got short-changed on this and am determined to make a big deal of it.

It bothers me that my voice is not deeper in tone and that people think I am a female on the phone. I observe other men in dressing rooms and compare myself with them, weighing my masculine traits against theirs, and I am always inadequate in comparison.

I do not consider this worry to be homosexuality. I do not want to have relations with men; I only want to observe them. I feel if only I could sit and observe them for one whole day in a locker room, I would see the vast differences in the traits I have mentioned, and my anxiety would go away.

I choose to use the sneaky technique of comparing to make me feel bad about what I do have. I choose to see how I am "different" in other ways to help support this SDB. I choose to do this comparing, knowing that I can do it in such a way as to always appear inadequate. I get some kind of pleasure out of watching them and hurting myself. Why not choose to focus on my strong points?

I am happily married; I have children, and I love my wife very much. We have very good sexual relations. I get excited by *Playboy,* but this complex keeps nagging me. I questioned my doctor about a hormonal deficiency, but he said that as long as I have adequate sexual responses in marriage, I am normal.

I am no homosexual. I am normal. I am all male.

I can believe him and not let it bug me anymore, but I have chosen not to yet.

I tell myself if only I had larger genitals and hair on my chest I would feel adequate and that if my father had taken a greater interest in me to help me be more athletic, I would feel adequate.

I choose to keep these ifs going rather than accept the way things really are and go on from there.

I choose to believe that adequacy is dependent on size, and this is an irrational belief. Adequacy is not in size. The genital organ is not any more functional nor masculine if it is large. "Normal" comes in all sizes, not just large. A small one may have some advantages over a large one; it has a greater percentage of volume increase than a large one. Do I use these ways of thinking about myself so that I can hide behind them and not really test out my adequacy as a male? Do I erroneously think that hair on the chest has anything to do with strength, agility, skill, or intelligence? Am I using this no-hair bit as a cop-out to keep me from being and doing what I actually could be and do?

Tuesday
I am having a very hard time making myself analyze my SDB pattern. I am trying to put too many other activities in the way so that I can defeat the program for myself. But I feel a little lighter just having let the problem out into the open. I feel I am paying some big and heavy prices; one is that I feel so dumb even worrying about outward signs of masculinity.

Intellectually, I know that such signs do not designate the masculine and unmasculine. Somehow I worry that *others* are doubting my masculinity. I know I function well as a husband and father, but it seems important to me that other men recognize this too. Intellectually, I know that others are too wrapped up in their own problems to be concerned about me. So why am I concerned about what they think of me? I miss a great deal of things going on around me by breaking my neck to observe chest hair on others. This preoccupation prevents me from seeing, talking about, or thinking about many other interesting and more worthwhile topics. It is a compulsion with me.

I am trying to defeat the program for myself to keep the SDB pattern going and to continue to pay the prices for doing so. Already, just getting this out into the open to myself has helped me feel better about myself. Great, this is progress; keep going! I know all this, but my feelings tell me some other message. I choose to do the thinking for others. I can choose to let them think what they will and not be so responsible for whatever they choose to think. After all, they have SDBs too.

I am concerned about what I think of me and choose to project these feelings into others to continue to react toward them in nonsocial nonaccepting ways. It is I who does not accept me, not they. When I learn to accept me as is and that God created my body whole and complete for its purposes, I will find it easier to accept others and to be accepted by others.

185

Being so busy doing my SDB keeps me from developing new friendships or relationships and makes me feel less than in complete control of my life. I have also noticed that when I am busy at work, the behavior leaves, but when an idle moment comes, the SDB returns.

I was not aware of how unhappy this anxiety makes me until I started thinking about it in this program. I had considered it just a trivial worry, but now I can see that I *must* get rid of these feelings.

Saturday

My SDB made me browse through magazines today at the barbershop. I was in search of photos of shirtless men. I envy those men with a display of muscular physiques and chest hair.

I am still making myself notice men around me with a great deal of chest hair. They may be working in their yards, driving by me, or whatever, and I make myself notice them and compare myself with them.

When I catch myself doing this, I engage in an intellectual battle: chest hair has no relationship to masculinity. But somehow I make myself feel that it does.

Then I fantasize on how much more masculine, respected, outgoing, happy I would be with the development of hair on my chest.

I also realize how stupid this is, but I make myself unhappy over the lack of it, anyway. And I

It is going to be great, just being me.

I use it to stop myself from doing this. I can choose to make new friends in spite of it. I seem not to want to take the responsibility for the doing of it when I say the "SDB returns." It cannot "return." I do it, or it won't get done!

I had before managed to hide it under the rug, walk over the lump, and keep on kidding myself that it is of no real consequence; but now that I examine it closer, it is of consequence and it must go!

As far as being in control of my life, who is? I am, even when I make myself feel I am out of control.

I am disowning here. Do I tell myself that I am not responsible for what I am choosing to do? Do I consider this SDB as something outside of myself and therefore not in my control? I purposely choose to look for these visual cues to help me set off my feeling about myself, and it works. I am catching myself when I do all this, and now I am about ready to choose to not do it.

I seem determined to get something out of this looking and comparing deal; otherwise, why would I continue to do it even when I know it is getting to be a drag? And the prices I pay are not worth it.

186

make myself believe that other men are looking down on me because of my lack. I make myself feel that they are doubting my masculinity.

But I have received a taste of what a relief, almost a joy, it will be to be free of my SDB. I am beginning to realize that I make myself act in this self-defeating way. I have the power to stop this behavior!

Sunday

I am becoming more conscious of the outer choices I make to maintain my SDB. I look at sports magazines not because of an interest in sports but because I will see men there with what I consider masculine traits. I route my driving to and from work by construction sites for the same reason. I enter a dressing room not just for the purpose of observing others, but I know that the opportunity to do so will be there.

It is an impossibility to go day to day without meeting a situation wherein opportunities to do my SDB are available. The solution is to drop the SDB, not the situations, although I can change some of those out-of-the-way ones.

I can control my outer choices! I went swimming today and decided that all of those traits about which I worry are insignificant. I forced my-

I forget that even people with hair of great amounts on their chests also have SDBs and may not be outgoing, friendly, or respected because of them. It has got to be an irrational way of thinking I engage in to keep this SDB going.

Here I am doing their feeling and thinking for them. This only gets back to who is really doing the feeling and looking down. It's me! I am my own worst critic and enemy.

I am catching on! I am in control over all that I do, think, and feel! And especially what I choose to look at.

I am making more and more progress!

When I choose to go on the SDB route, I am choosing at the same time all the consequences and results along that route. I am becoming more aware of the inner choices I make to keep my SDB going by these outer choices in the physical world around me and by the interpretation I place on other people. I am in charge of this interpretation. I have been choosing to let it hurt me. Now I can see that more clearly than before.

187

self not to observe others. I feel very satisfied with myself for this and the success I had.

It is a cycle. I control outer SDB choices and feel more masculine, which makes it easier to control the SDB. There must be a better way than "will power" to control a SDB. I am searching for my inner choice. That may help me find the better way.

Excellent. Victory does taste great.

Very good insight. Will power is nothing more than time and agency. I therefore have as much of both as anyone else has. I have moments of time given to me in which I am free to choose my own directions. Either the SDB route or the non-SDB route are always open, and the situation at the fork in the road will present itself many times a day.

Monday

I find a new sense of freedom in controlling my outer choices. I am pleased to be in control of situations, instead of letting them control me. I now find that I want to know the "why" of my SDB. What made me tie myself up in all those doubts?

Clearing up some outward SDB choices has given me a desire to participate in sports, something I have not done because of fear of competition. I am also recognizing masculine traits within myself which I had hidden from myself with this SDB.

I still cannot identify the inner choice that leads to my SDB. Because of this, I fear that my SDB will return and that I am merely using will power to control outer choices.

Great progress. I am discovering that I am indeed in control over this SDB. Now I want to dig deeper to see what is behind all this.

I do not need to hide behind my SDB and use it as a cop-out any more! I am discovering myself. What a great feeling! I am likely to turn out more masculine than I had ever thought I was or could be as I get down to the real me behind this SDB. It is very simple now. My inner choice was to keep me feeling inadequate as a male so that I could have a legitimate reason for not entering into competitive situations with other men. All this was dictated by the fear of looking foolish if I should fail to be perfect in those situations. All the other things I have been doing, such as looking at other men, instead of actually doing what it takes to get those muscles, were done as a cheating way to achieve masculinity. Taking action is the way to build such skills and muscles, not looking, imagining, or fantasizing. These are only mental short-cuts and cheat us out of the real thing.

I had also been choosing not to test how really adequate I am as a male, and these other techniques and outer choices helped to keep me from such a test.

Tuesday

I find it easier and easier to control outer choices, but I still cannot pinpoint my inner choice. I try to figure it out and find my mind wandering. Perhaps I am *avoiding* defining the inner choice rather than just *unable* to define it.

This seems to be an avoidance technique to keep me from looking too closely at what is appearing to be the truth of the matter.

Great insight.

Maybe I fear finding myself inadequate; so I use my SDB to keep me from testing my adequacy. I tell myself "you are really adequate, but your SDB tells you you're not adequate." I think maybe I hang onto the SDB rather than test myself by forming friendships and participating in sports.

Right on!
My old label is still trying to hang in there and be in control over what I tell myself. But now I am seeing through this whole game.

Great thinking! Now we are getting someplace.

I feel good about beating the outward displays of this SDB, but I fear that inner problems will lead me to other SDBs. (Printed by permission.)

This is a mythical fear I conjure up to help scare me into keeping my old SDB pattern. I can recognize it as a fear, not a reality, and act accordingly. [Note: Many people fear developing other SDBs to take the place of the one about to bite the dust. But this does not happen unless they go all out to create a new one. And even doing this is very difficult in face of all they now know about this kind of behavior. It takes all the fun out of starting a new one.]

Now I can test out my abilities to be my best

friendly self. I can let people
get close to me and really
know me. They will like what
they find, for I was created
whole and complete. I have
used this SDB to keep
people away from me long
enough! World, here I come!

The following letter was addressed to me twenty-seven days after the last daily diary entry from George W. This was also twenty-seven days after the conclusion of the ESDB workshop in which George was enrolled.

August 15, 1973

Dear Dr. Chamberlain,

I just want to thank you for letting me participate in your SDB workshop. I can't believe the change it has made in me. Even my wife has noticed a difference, but she doesn't know what it is.

I still have some problems, but I feel so much more free to work on those problems. When I dropped those doubts of my masculinity, you can't imagine what a sense of relief I felt. I think I know what joy is now. To think that I let myself carry that heavy weight for so long a time!

This has really been a learning experience this summer. Your SDB workshop has been one of the most worthwhile and enjoyable classes I have ever had. It was the "extra" learnings that made it so.

Well, thank you so very much. You have made me a happier person than I could have imagined and have changed me more than you will ever know.

Sincerely,

George W.

About the Author

As a teacher of teenagers, Jonathan Chamberlain felt frustrated when students came to him for counseling concerning their personal problems. In an effort to become more knowledgeable, he began training in counseling in summer school at Brigham Young University. Later, with a scholarship for further training in guidance and counseling, he attended the University of Wyoming, where he obtained his masters degree—then, in 1967, his Ph.D. in psychology and counselor education, all the while supporting his wife and five children.

Finding that positions for psychologists in universities had been filled, Dr. Chamberlain accepted a government-funded position for one summer with Program Headstart in southeastern Utah, counseling and evaluating four-year-old Navajo children. When government funds were depleted for that position, he found another as a school psychologist in Price, Utah, for a five-school-district project serving 12,000 children who had never had counseling. There he became director of The Regional Child Study Services covering one-fourth of the state of Utah. Again government funds ran out, and in 1970 he was offered a position at the Brigham Young University counseling center, where he had desired to work. He has been happy in his work at BYU and in his private practice as a licensed psychologist and marriage and family counselor.

Recalling his experiences with the Navajo children, Dr. Chamberlain cites the great need of the children's parents for help of the right kind. There on the Navajo reservation he met his first four-year-old alcoholic, who many mornings staggered drunk into the classroom. The parents of the little boy spent their welfare allotment on liquor for themselves and their children. One four-year-old Navajo girl unsuccessfully attempted to keep her six-month-old brother alive by feeding him leaves. Dr. Chamberlain's job was partly to search out these neglected children, work with their parents, and, where necessary, report them to the state welfare agency, who took the children away for more adequate care.

Some of the children in the Navajo Headstart program had never seen a mirror and did not realize they were seeing themselves when it was held before their faces. They could name everyone else in the classroom, but when they viewed themselves and the teacher asked, "who is that?" they would say, "I don't know. I never saw him (or her) before." Dr. Chamberlain and the Headstart teacher helped these children learn how to use knives, forks, and spoons and how to brush their teeth for the first time—also to use books, crayons, and other educational tools they had never seen. The parents of these children loved their little ones, Dr. Chamberlain says, but alcoholism was a sickness too compelling for some, and it created many tragedies.

"The white man came to help the Indians," says Dr. Chamberlain; "since that time, they have been largely unhelped. Of 160 government programs for the Indians, few have done much for them. The dole program took away their dignity, and they want it back. Humans need to be in control of their own lives as much as possible."

That is what he likes about his work at BYU and his private practice: his clients do their own work, with his help. Almost every day he sees people being successful at overcoming a self-defeating behavior. The interesting thing to him about his "overcoming-self-defeating-behavior" program is that his colleagues "took it as a joke" at first and chaffed him about it unmercifully. He pursued it, however, convinced of its possibilities for helping people overcome their behavior problems. Although the program is different from the usual psychological work—different, even, from Dr. Chamberlain's own training—results are often remarkable.

Some of his success stories with the self-defeating-behavior program include helping male patients overcome sexual problems—homosexuality in particular. He has attended the heterosexual marriages of three former homosexuals.

He is quick to add, however, that some of his clients fail in this program—out of lack of motivation or the fear of becoming responsible for their own actions. But the successes more than compensate for the failures.

Dr. Chamberlain met his future bride while on a mission for The Church of Jesus Christ of Latter-day Saints. For 2½ years they courted by mail while he served in the U.S. Air Force; then after two dates they were married. In his earlier years he was a journeyman carpenter with his twin brother and an older brother in southern California. When he was seventeen, in a nine-month period, working many hours a day with only two laborers helping them, they built five small homes, a mansion for a movie star, a grocery store, and an eight-family apartment house. The ethic of hard work Dr. Chamberlain learned on the family ranch and dairy farm and from his church has paid off. He still works hard, but at a different kind of labor—a labor of love and satisfaction—helping people make progress in overcoming personality problems.

Looking toward the future, Dr. Chamberlain plans to develop the eliminating-self-defeating-behavior program on video disc and on video tape for the deaf and the blind. His home-study course in the subject will also reach past prison walls to help people there. And he plans to remain busy helping other psychologists and their clients learn of the program, in these ways making his contribution to the world.

The possibilities for the "eliminating-self-defeating-behaviors" program, says Dr. Chamberlain, are unlimited.